Those of us working in palliative care know how managing psychological and spiritual pain can often be far more challenging than managing physical pain. This is especially the case when our patients do not know what awaits them, if anything, after they die. I am convinced that *Dying to Live – Reflections on Life After Death* will be a big help to many, giving them comfort and filling them with hope and purpose in this difficult phase of their life.

Dr Jacob Kwak, MBBS, FRACP, FAChPM

Palliative Medicine Physician, Blacktown and Adventist Hospitals, Sydney

John Flader's book *Dying to Live – Reflections on Life After Death* is a must-read for those in any doubt about life after death. There are some sobering lines such as 'What happens after we die does not depend on what we personally think it is going to be'. The studies by my colleague, Dr Jeffrey Long, M.D., another radiation oncologist, on almost five thousand near-death experiences, adds a wealth of data. I will be recommending this book to my patients.

Prof. Gerald B. Fogarty BSc, MBBS, PhD, FRANZCR (FRO)

Oncologist, St Vincent's Hospital, Sydney; Professor, Monash University; Professor, University of Technology, Sydney

For those who are wondering whether there is life after death, or who do not believe in it, this book is superb. In an informal, easy-to-read style, it examines evidence from multiple sources for life after death, filling the reader with hope in the potential of the human being to transcend himself and live on. It addresses the great questions of life, answering them with skill and precision, and it invites further reflection. Essential reading for a time of change.

Prof. José Perez Adán, PhD

Professor of Sociology, University of Valencia, Spain

D1446951

This little book takes into account the views of eminent philosophers and scientists on what happens when we die – and we shall all die. In particular, the author deals with the so-called scientific objections, such as those from Stephen Hawking who, as the Jesuit astronomer Guy Consolmagno has pointed out, 'is a brilliant physicist and when it comes to theology, I can say he is a brilliant physicist'! This book argues, not from authority as so many of us are tempted to do when challenged by the ultimate questions, but from common sense distinctions, powerful because of their simplicity, which deal with why we exist, an issue which confronts every human at some stage. 'Since God is ultimately the answer to these deeper questions, we are really seeking God all along, whether we look at it that way or not.' I highly recommend this very readable book!

Prof. Tony Shannon, PhD, AM

Emeritus Professor of Mathematics, University of Technology, Sydney

This book couldn't have come at a more opportune time. The past two years have seen people all over the world having close encounters with the death of loved ones resulting from COVID-19. Whether they believe in a religion or have no religion at all, they will find in this book a rational answer to the all-important question of what happens to a human being after death. The natural light of reason shed by this book could even lead to a radical change in some people's behaviour during the remaining years of their life.

Prof. Bernardo M. Villegas, PhD (Harvard),

Professor of Economics, University of Asia and the Pacific, Manila, Philippines

DYING TO LIVE

Reflections on

LIFE AFTER DEATH

John Flader

Connor Court Publishing

Published in 2022 by Connor Court Publishing Pty Ltd

Connor Court Publishing Pty Ltd
PO Box 7257
Redland Bay QLD 4165
sales@connorcourt.com
www.connorcourt.com

Printed in Australia

ISBN: 9781922449979

Front cover designed by Mathew De Sousa

Bible citations from the The Revised Standard Version, Second Catholic Edition.

For Ellie, who was diagnosed with brain cancer at the age of fifteen, who firmly believed in life after death and looked forward to it with great longing, and who died at the age of twenty on the day I finished writing this book. May she rest in peace.

Table of Contents

Foreword

Time is short. Most readers of this book will be in the last quarter of their lives, perhaps the last ten or five percent. The very end of life is for most not an ideal time for serious thinking, as major health problems affect concentration. Ideally, the time for re-evaluating one's assumptions about life after death is now – this week, not "in the next few years when I get around to it".

Unfortunately, most people bring to the end of their lives the opinions they took on quickly and insouciantly in their teens, when death was a long way off. Often those views were the unexamined assumptions of wider society; for example, that death is the end and science sees no evidence of anything beyond. That might turn out to be true. But it would be wise to examine the evidence with the capacity for reflection that comes from long experience of life. This book lays out the evidence for life after death clearly, rigorously and (as the reader convinced of the urgency of the case will appreciate) succinctly, without wasting time.

The reasons for believing in life after death come from three converging directions. First, there is direct evidence from those who have had near-death experiences and from alleged appearances from those who have died. Second, philosophical reflection on the nature of the mind can suggest it is the kind of thing that could have, and in fact does have, a separate and immortal existence. Thirdly, immortality is a tenet of overall Christian belief, which is itself supported by a range of evidence, from arguments for the existence of God to scriptural texts.

What will surprise readers of this book is that the evidence for life after death has become considerably stronger in their own lifetimes. It has done so in all three of those dimensions.

By around 1950, spiritualism and its hopes for voices from "the other side" speaking in séances had been discredited; so had any prospect of accepting theories of reincarnation. Only anecdotal accounts of near-death experiences existed. But in the decades since then, as the author describes in riveting detail, the resources of modern medicine have been brought to bear. Medical advances have meant that many patients can now be brought back "from the brink" after heart attacks and can tell us what they experienced. Doctors who have become fascinated by the phenomenon have devoted resources to collecting, recording and analysing the thousands of accounts, and finding many commonalities in the stories. We now have the beginnings of a properly scientific overview of an aspect of reality barely suspected only decades ago.

Also around 1950, psychology and philosophy of mind reached a low point, with behaviourist orthodoxy maintaining that the brain was a complex stimulus-response system with nothing really mental in there – no "ghost in the machine". Philosophers of mind had lost sight of the insights, well described in this book, of earlier thinkers like Aristotle, Avicenna and Aquinas, who saw the difficulty of fitting true understanding into a materialist view of the mind. The mid-century's simplistic philosophy of mind led to rash promises of Artificial Intelligence at human level within a few years. But the history of psychology, cognitive science and artificial intelligence in the decades since has seen a massive retreat from those positions. Trying to imitate thinking showed how hard it is. And it is especially understanding that is hard to imitate: a little experience with mistakes in Google Translate quickly makes the point that its data processing powers are amazing but there's no-one in there understanding language. It has become recognised too that consciousness is a hard problem, not easily explained away in materialist terms. Contemporary philosophy of mind is very diverse and much less dismissive of claims for the unique and possibly spiritual nature of mind.

Many brash scientists of the 1950s believed themselves on the point of creating intelligence in a machine and life in a test tube and thus once and for all exorcising mind and God from the world. What would have most surprised them is that a development in physics would support arguments for the existence of God. (Physics?! *Et tu, Brute?*) Quite unexpectedly, it came to be realised that the constants of the universe were "fine-tuned": only if the basic numbers like the strength of the gravitational force were extremely close to their actual values could the universe have developed planets capable of supporting life. And "extremely close" does not mean within a few percent, it means correct to something like one part in 10^{40}. This book explains these extraordinary facts very clearly. Coincidence? The whole methodology of modern statistics is to rule out as unbelievable theories that require massive coincidences. Perhaps future developments in physics will cast a different light on the question, but as of 2022, the state of physics renders unlikely the theory of a chance origin of the universe, or of the origin of life, for that matter.

Even with the other arm of evidence for Christianity, the scriptural texts, matters are clearer than in 1950. At that time Biblical studies were still affected by the German "higher criticism" of the previous century which argued that most of the Gospel story was made up by the early Christian faith community to explain its faith commitment. We have more experience with interpreting texts now. It has become clearer that the Gospels are much as would be expected from well-informed reporters a few decades after the events.

It is timely to bring this knowledge together – timely both from the point of view of the new state of the knowledge and from the point of view of the needs of inquirers into the burning question of life after death, who have little time to spare. John Flader has done his readers a great service.

Now turn the page and read the book.

Don't leave it too long. I am confident you will be pleasantly surprised with what you find.

James Franklin, PhD
Honorary Professor of Mathematics and Statistics, University of New South Wales, Sydney
Author of *Corrupting the Youth: A History of Philosophy in Australia*

Introduction

This book was not my idea. It came as a suggestion from a friend who proposed a book for people who are nearing the end of life and are wondering what happens after they die. He was thinking especially of people without any religion or belief in God, or at least of people without any active practice of a religion they might have had before. He had in mind mainly people who are getting old and are wondering about life after death. It should answer those questions so many people ask: Is there life after death? How do we know? If there is life, what sort of life is it?

But it is not only the elderly who are nearing the end. There are many younger people too, and even very young people, who are suffering from a terminal illness and are asking the same questions.

And, of course, it is not only people without any religious belief. People who have followed some religion – it doesn't matter what religion that might be – usually have some idea of what awaits them, but they may want clearer answers, and more certainty, about them.

So that is how this book came to be. And that is what it proposes to do – to answer those questions about life after death.

When my friend came up with the suggestion, I immediately became enthused. After all, I too am nearing the end. What is more, I have thought a lot about the matter over the years, I have read books about it, and I have written quite a few articles about it. Plus, I too know a good number of people who are asking those questions, and who don't know the answers.

The outline of the book is simple. On the assumption that most of the readers do not have any religion or belief in God, the book starts from what we can know by reason alone to show that there has to be life after death, whether we believe in it or not. Also, using mainly arguments drawn from contemporary findings about the universe, we address the question of whether there is a God whom we might meet "on the other side".

A key chapter is that on what have come to be called near-death experiences, where a person has suffered severe trauma, usually with a cardiac arrest, and, while unconscious, feels their soul leave the body and go, variously, through a number of stages. These include the soul hovering above the body and observing what is happening below, going through a tunnel to a bright light and a heavenly experience, seeing their whole life in an instant, and, in a few cases, having a hellish experience. All of this points to the existence of various states of life after death.

Then, for those who say that no one has ever come back from the dead to tell us about it, we look at instances in which people have indeed come back from the dead and have appeared on earth to tell us about it.

Since all these experiences are totally consistent with the Christian understanding of life after death, we consider how it is eminently reasonable to examine the Christian view on the question, since it is a very comprehensive body of teaching which has been developed over the last two thousand years. We then study the principal aspects of life after death from this perspective. Naturally, it is not expected that the reader will be Christian or have any desire to become Christian.

And finally, we suggest ways in which the reader, no matter what religious belief they may have, can prepare for their own death with hope and confidence.

When all is said and done, the question of life after death is one of the most important ones anyone can ask. It concerns the very purpose and meaning of life. How we come to answer it determines how we live here – and hereafter. It can mean the difference between living with fear and dread of what happens when we die, and of looking forward to it with hope and joy. In short, it makes all the difference in the world. And it affects not only our own life but the lives of those around us.

When I told a friend about the book I was writing, he immediately became enthused. He said that most of the friends with whom he went to school, a Christian school at that, no longer have any religion or belief in God, and some of them are dying from terminal illnesses, quite unprepared for what awaits them. He wanted copies of the book as soon as it was published so that he could give them copies.

He then told me the story of his father, whose life was totally transformed by someone who knew where he was going when he died. His father was one of Sydney's leading surgeons, and an honorary surgeon at two major hospitals. His prestige led him to be named head of a team of medical specialists who were on call whenever a very important person, like the Queen of England or an American President, went to Sydney. Although he was raised a Congregationalist and attended a Church of England school before going to university, he had no personal relationship with God.

One day in the late 1950s when he was driving his three sons to school, he stopped at a hospital to visit a patient on whom he had recently performed an operation. The man had cancer of the stomach and he wasn't expected to live long. When the doctor returned to the car after the visit, the boys saw that he was very emotional, something they had never seen in him, and they asked him what had happened.

He told them that when he walked into the room, the patient put down his paper and greeted him with a big smile and said, "Doctor, I know it's not normally done, but I want you to be honest with me and please give me an indication of how long I have to live." The doctor, with some hesitation, told him possibly six to twelve weeks, but this could vary, depending on the circumstances.

The patient then smiled broadly and thanked him, as if relieved by the news. The doctor was astounded. He had never seen such a reaction to what he considered the equivalent of a death sentence. He was more used to hearing something along the lines of, "If there is a God, please help me, and don't let me die." He asked the patient the reason for his joy-filled response, and the answer dumbfounded him: "Well Doctor, I know where I am going and now you have given me a timeline, so I can get my affairs in order and prepare to meet my maker".

The experience greatly affected the doctor and moved him, along with his wife, to set about growing in their relationship with God. Soon afterwards, they attended a rally conducted by the Evangelist Billy Graham, where they committed themselves to Jesus Christ. The doctor became an elder in the Presbyterian Church, and he and his wife began to rise early each morning to read the Bible and have a quiet time of prayer. Their new faith had a lasting impact on their children and on many others as well.

So yes, the question of what happens when we die is important. This book proposes to shed light on the question, basing itself on reason, on human experience and on what God himself has told us. It is my hope that those who read it will find answers to their own questions, and that they will be able to look towards their own death with hope and peace.

1

Nearing the end

When you get to my age – I was born in the 1940s – you spend a lot of time attending funerals. Sometimes they are of younger people, but most of the time they are of people more or less of your same age – your friends, relatives, workmates, acquaintances... People in the so-called "twilight years" of life.

It's part of life – and death. But it also means you are running out of friends and, what is more, of tennis, golfing, fishing and bridge partners. Of course, you can always read, watch television, do the gardening or engage in some charitable work, which can also be very fulfilling.

At this stage of life, your thoughts turn more and more to deeper, and perhaps more troubling, questions. When is it going to be my turn? When will the funeral be mine, and it will be my relatives and friends who do the mourning? Have I provided sufficiently for those I leave behind? How hard will it be to say goodbye? Have I forgiven someone who has hurt me a long time ago? Have I been reconciled with that brother or sister, or even that son or daughter whom I haven't seen or even heard from for many years?

It's troubling, but in some sense easy, to think about these things and, in the end, you don't have to worry about what happens after you die. Someone else will look after your affairs.

Your thoughts also turn to the distant past, to the whole of your life. Your childhood, your family life in those early years, the love you experienced when you were growing up, your schooling, your many accomplishments. And then what you did after school: further study, your job, your marriage, your children, your middle age and now your advancing years. Many happy memories, and perhaps a few sad, even troubling, ones. A life well lived, but inevitably some regrets too. That's normal.

And more philosophical questions. The uniqueness of your life: that there was only one of you, with your family, your talents, your relationships. Why do I exist at all? Why did my life take the twists and turns it did? Was it just chance or fate, or was it somehow meant to be? When all is said and done, does life have meaning? Or am I just a cork tossed about on the waves of fate, destined to sink one day to the bottom of the ocean, never to be seen again?

Surely, you think, there must be more to life than that. It can't be totally meaningless. There must be some meaning, some purpose, at least in your relationships with others. After all, you have had an impact on the many people with whom you have come in contact over the years. Those many others have somehow benefitted from knowing you. At least you hope so. Can't you live on somehow in their memory and in the various ways you have helped them?

And, looking at the bigger picture, how small all of mankind is, and especially each individual, on this tiny planet we call Earth, lost in one galaxy among the hundreds of billions in this vast universe. Is all of this just an accident? How did it start? And how did it get to where it is today? Why does it have so much order, purpose and beauty? Did it perhaps have a creator, a designer?

What is more, each of us, this particular individual that we are, is somehow special. We are not just a higher animal, a bit more intelligent than one of the higher apes. After all, we can think, plan for the future, build houses, write poetry and music... There is something special about us humans that distinguishes us from all other living creatures.

And then those really serious questions that begin to absorb our thoughts more and more, and that perhaps we would rather not think about. But they won't go away. The big one is simple: What is on the other side? Is there life after death? Or is death the end and you just cease to exist? Or maybe you fall asleep forever, and never wake up?

Is there possibly a God, who created this universe and who created you, whom you are going to meet one day? Is there, as many people believe, a judgment where all will be laid bare and there will be no hiding? Then again, is there possibly a state of great joy with God, which people call heaven? If there is a God, what sort of being is he?

These are questions that keep popping up and that you really need to face. You can put them aside or run away from them, afraid of the answers. But they won't go away. There is reality out there. Either there is life after death or there isn't. Either you continue to exist, aware of your surroundings, or you cease to exist altogether. Either there is a God or there isn't. You wouldn't want to avoid the question only to find out, when it was too late, that you were wrong.

The purpose of this little book, as you think about the finish line of life, is to explore these questions. I am not going to impose anything on you. I respect your judgment and your freedom too much for that. I would like this book to be simply a quiet conversation about these important issues, where you ask the questions and I try to answer them.

I will answer them starting from reason itself, borne out by the experience of many people over the centuries. After all, this approach has found what I consider convincing answers to the deep questions of life and death. I think the answers are worth considering, even if you may not agree with all of them. They may at least help you understand the issues better so you can form your own judgment about them.

Perhaps our conversation will be something like the one I had on an airplane some time ago with a pleasant, recently married young man who described himself as an atheist. We chatted in a very quiet, friendly way for the whole duration of an hour and a half flight to another city. Among the questions he asked was: "What's your take on life after death?" I told him without a moment's hesitation, "I'm looking forward to it!" He was wearing a seat belt so he couldn't jump out of his seat, but I suspect he had never heard that before. After all, I have thought a lot about the question over the years and I have found answers that I consider convincing. I am indeed looking forward to it. I think most of us would be, or we would at least be hoping for some sort of happy existence after we die.

When we got off the plane and walked to the terminal, the young man thanked me for the conversation, which he said he had enjoyed very much, as I had. Then he added: "But I don't agree with anything you said." Fine.

2

Placing a bet

As we considered in the last chapter, the question of whether there is life after death is important. Very important. Many people put off thinking about it for a long time, but when they get closer to the end, the question inevitably returns, imposing itself with ever greater urgency. Is there life after death or not? Is there a God or not? It's really something like placing a bet. You can bet that there is a God and life after death or there isn't. One of those two is correct. But in this bet, everything is at stake. If there isn't anything on the other side, you haven't lost anything, because there was nothing to lose. Life just ends. But if there is life after death and you bet that there isn't, you've lost a great deal. This is one bet you can't afford to lose. The stakes are too high.

In the seventeenth century, Blaise Pascal (1623-1662), the famous French mathematician, physicist, inventor and philosopher, posed the question of the bet we are considering. He was writing for the sceptics of his own day to help them consider the possibilities – and the consequences – of the wager that there is, or there is not, a God, and with God life after death. His argument, commonly known as "Pascal's wager", comes in his *Pensées,* or *Thoughts.* His argument is well worth considering. A summary of it goes like this.

Either there is a God – and life after death – or there isn't. Pascal says that reason cannot decide between the two. He says this because he is writing for sceptics, who think that by reason alone one cannot know whether there is a God. Actually, as we will see later, human reason can know that there is a God. But let us continue with Pascal.

Human life, then, is like a game, in which in the end there is a God and life after death or there isn't. It's like tossing a coin, which will come up heads or tails. Heads means there is a God and, if you have lived and died well, you live happily ever after with him in indescribable bliss. Tails means there is no God and your life comes to an end. You must place a bet, you must decide how you are going to live. It is not optional. That is, you are going to die sooner or later and you will have to live with the consequences of your choice.

In fact, we could add, people do wager. Many believe in God and strive to live accordingly, making an effort to live a good moral life. Others believe there is no God and don't worry about morality or about what happens when they die. They will just cease to exist, so they think – and hope. Some of these people, nonetheless, "hedge their bets" and endeavour to live a decent life "just in case".

Let us first consider the consequences if we bet that there is a God and life after death, and so we strive to live a good life. If we win and there is a God, we gain everything. We bet the short life we live on earth, trying to live it well, and we gain union with God for all eternity in heaven. If we lose and there is no God, we haven't lost anything. We simply cease to exist after living a good life here on earth. So, betting on God offers the chance to gain everything and lose nothing.

Or we can bet that there is no God, no life after death, that when we die that's it – we simply cease to exist. It's all over. Then, as many who do not believe in God will do, we may fall more readily into self-indulgence, self-centredness, dishonesty, pride, laziness, etc. If we win and there is no God, we gain nothing, because there is nothing to gain. There is no life after death. But if we lose and there is a God and life after death, we miss out on the reward of eternal happiness with him in heaven. We lose everything. Everything. And of course, although Pascal doesn't say it, this can also mean we end up suffering for all eternity in hell. Yes, hell. It exists, whether we believe in it or not. We'll see more about that later.

It is clear from this argument that it would be foolish indeed to bet that there is no God and no life after death. There is nothing to gain and everything to lose, whereas betting that there is a God promises everything to gain and nothing to lose.

One person who went through this very reasoning process in the early 1980s was the then 24-year-old New Zealander, Ian McCormack. He relates in a testimony on YouTube (https://www.youtube.com/watch?v=Yg4188Ii-fg) how he was diving one night off the coast of Mauritius, when he felt a strong stinging on his arm. He discovered that he had been stung by a box jellyfish, and by the time he got out of the water he had been stung five times. He knew these jellyfish can kill a person in ten to fifteen minutes. His arm quickly swelled to twice its size and he was becoming progressively paralysed and drowsy. He says: "I was dying. If I don't make it and die before I get to the hospital, what would happen to me? Is there life after death, or when a man dies, is that it? Finished. Cessation of life. Well, as a heathen, as an atheist, I reckoned when you died it was all over. The trouble was, I wasn't sure. You can be wrong. I was a gambler and I'm gambling with my life here. If I'm gambling and I'm wrong here, I'm gambling; it's like Russian roulette. I could be wrong here. I have no idea what would happen to me if I died."

On his way to hospital in an ambulance he somehow saw before his eyes the words of the Lord's Prayer, "Forgive us our trespasses". It moved him to beg God to forgive his many sins. Upon arrival at the hospital he passed out and appeared to have died, remaining unconscious for fifteen minutes. During that time his soul left his body and went first to hell, which he realised he would have deserved had he not begged God to forgive his sins. Then he experienced heaven, with its unimaginable joy, such that he would have preferred not to return to life on earth. But when he considered that if he remained in heaven his mother would have spent the rest of her life worrying that her son had gone to hell, he was eager to return. He recovered and his life was changed forever.

We can learn a lot from his experience. Facing what he thought could very well be imminent death, he took the question of life after death seriously. He realised that what would happen to him if he died did not depend on what he, as an atheist, thought might happen. There was life after death or there wasn't. If there was, he was not prepared for it and that thought frightened him.

But there is more to it than what awaits us after death. It is important to remember that those who live a good life find great happiness already here on earth. They will fail often, as we all do, but the very effort to be kind, generous, honest, hardworking, loyal, brings its own reward. People who live a good life are respected and loved by others, and they find great peace and joy. Pascal puts it like this: "But what harm will come to you from taking this course [committing to God]? You will be faithful, honest, humble, grateful, doing good, a sincere, true friend. It is true you will not enjoy noxious pleasures, glory and good living. But will you not have others? I tell you that you will gain even in this life".

Conversely, those who disregard God's law and the good of others may have a comfortable existence, perhaps even make a lot of money and have many enjoyments, but they do not have the deep peace of soul that the others do. As C.S. Lewis says in his book *The Great Divorce,* which is an allegory on heaven and hell, those who go to heaven begin their heaven on earth and those who go to hell begin their hell on earth.

So independently of what awaits us in the next life, already in this life we reap the rewards of betting that there is life after death and living our lives accordingly. If we bet that there is no life after death, we may not be as happy in this life and we may suffer for all eternity in the next.

It is clear which is the better wager.

3

The soul

Many will argue that they don't believe in life after death, whether there is a God or not. We will simply die and cease to exist and that's the end of it. They are entitled to their belief. But, as we have just seen, they might be wrong, and the consequences are enormous. And, what is more, they run up against a fact of nature that puts an end to the argument: the human soul.

What do we mean by a soul? A soul is the life principle of any living being. It is what distinguishes a living thing from a non-living one. Rocks, soil, water, atoms don't have souls. Plants, animals and humans do. It is the soul which gives life, unity to the living thing, making it function as a single entity. It integrates the organs and functions so that all work together to keep the being alive.

For example, in the case of a plant, while it is alive all of its parts – the roots, stem, leaves, flowers – work together to keep the plant alive, growing and able to reproduce itself. But because the plant soul – or the animal soul, for that matter – is not spiritual, when the plant dies the soul, the organising principle, ceases to exist and the various parts of the plant decay and disintegrate. The plant decomposes into the elements that make it up. The Greek philosopher Aristotle (384-322 BC) called the plant soul *bios*, from which we get the word biology. It is commonly called a vegetative soul, which gives unity to the plant and allows it to grow and reproduce.

In the case of animals, which are of a higher order than plants, the growth and reproductive functions of plants are there, but in addition the animal has the ability to move and to experience sensations. Aristotle called the animal soul *zoê,* from which we get the word zoology. The animal soul, or sensitive soul, includes the functions of the vegetative soul. But since the animal soul, like the plant soul, is not spiritual – it is just the unifying, organising principle of the animal – when the animal dies the soul ceases to exist and the animal decays and breaks up into its constituent elements. The animal simply is no more.

But when we come to humans, we find something completely different. In addition to the functions of reproduction and growth in plants, and those of movement and sensation in animals, humans have the ability to think, to plan, to reason. These are spiritual functions, in some way independent of matter. Aristotle called the human soul the *psūchê,* the psyche, from which we get the word psychology.

By its spiritual soul, the human person is radically different from animals, even from the highest apes. A person can think of a better way to do things, and so make progress over time. Humans invented a way to make fire, spears, bows and arrows, boomerangs, wheels, carts, internal combustion engines, motor vehicles, airplanes, rockets, and space craft capable of flying to the moon and back. Humans found ways to plant seeds and grow crops, cure illnesses with medicines, and make radios, television sets and computers. They developed language, and produced works of art, literature and music. Animals can't do this. They do not have a spiritual soul which allows them to think, to reason. They simply live the way they always have, following their instincts. They do not make progress. Birds always make their nests in the same way, spiders make their webs in the same way, chimpanzees mate and raise their offspring in the same way...

Yes, higher animals like dogs and especially apes, have what we can call the affective life: the emotions, the feelings. They show affection for their young, they play with one another, they appear to be happy or sad, angry or frightened. In this they can sometimes appear to be almost human. Since the human soul includes the functions of the vegetative soul of plants and the sensitive soul of animals, the human person has some functions in common with these lower beings. But that does not make animals human. It simply means that they have some functions in common with us and we humans have some functions in common with them.

Humans are radically different from the highest animals because our soul is spiritual. In addition to knowing material objects like food, cars and books, we humans can know and think about completely immaterial objects, like goodness, love, honesty and truth. A material being like a plant or animal cannot do this. Yes, we have a brain, as do animals, through which we know and think, but our soul is in some way independent of the brain, of a higher order than it, allowing us to understand and think about the immaterial, the spiritual. A material organ like the brain cannot by itself know something spiritual like goodness and love.

This reminds me of the story of the atheist professor of medicine who, having expertly dissected a corpse, triumphantly asked the class, "Now, where is the soul?" Whereupon a believing student quickly retorted that, if one could do the same with a living brain, he could ask, "Where is the thought?"

Avicenna (ca. 980-1037 AD), the Persian philosopher and physician, and a follower of Aristotle, came up with an argument to show how the human soul has existence in its own right, independently of the body. He asked people to imagine themselves suspended in the air, isolated from all sensations, with no contact even with their own body. He argued that a person in this situation would still have self-consciousness, self-awareness. He concluded that the self is not logically dependent on any physical thing and that, therefore, the soul is a substance with existence in its own right.

Thomas Aquinas (1225-1274), the great Italian philosopher and theologian, based his philosophy largely on that of Aristotle and he too argued that the soul was a spiritual substance. The soul, he said, can reflect, a term derived from the Latin, meaning to "bend back" on itself. It can know that it knows, think that it is thinking, reflect on its own activity. No material organ can do this. From this too we can see that the soul has existence in its own right, that it is a spiritual substance.

Pardon me if I have used philosophical language in this explanation but, when all is said and done, it is just common sense. It is what we observe when we reflect on life. And from this we conclude that if our spiritual soul has existence in its own right, it cannot die when the person dies. As a matter of fact, death is traditionally defined as the separation of the soul from the body. If you have ever been present when someone died, as I have, you have witnessed something profoundly mysterious. In one moment the person is alive and breathing. In the next the breathing stops, there is no more consciousness, and the person is dead. The soul has left the body. The body is lying there, motionless, but the soul is no longer there.

Because the soul is spiritual, without any matter, there is nothing that can destroy it. You can destroy something material, whether it be a house, a book, a car or even an atom, but you cannot destroy something spiritual. There is no matter to destroy. Of necessity it must continue to exist. What happens to it when the person dies, we shall see later. That is the whole purpose of this book.

If we want more evidence for the separate existence of the soul, we can look at the numerous accounts of near-death experiences, where a person has suffered severe trauma, like a cardiac arrest, and is clinically dead, before being resuscitated. During this time thousands of people have related later how their soul separated from their body and was watching their own resuscitation.

In one such case a man who had been in a deep coma later told a nurse that he recognised her and, when she was looking for his dentures, he told her where she had put them while he was unconscious. They were there, precisely where he said.

In another case an elderly woman who had suffered a cardiac arrest felt her soul leave the body, hover above it, and observe the resuscitation. After she was revived, she told one of the doctors how she had seen his pen fall from his pocket and how he had gone over to pick it up near the window, where her soul was watching. The doctor was amazed. What is more, and truly extraordinary, is that the woman was blind, but now, from her soul, she could see.

So yes, we have a spiritual soul, distinct from the body, and it continues to exist in a conscious state when we die. It doesn't just fade away into nothingness. It doesn't cease to exist. There is life after death, whether we believe in it or not.

4

Longing for what is beyond

Animals and plants, which are composed only of matter, by their very nature seek only what is material: food, water, protection from the elements, sunlight... Humans too, because we have a body, seek material things. But because we also have a spiritual soul with intelligence, the range of material things we seek is much broader. In addition to food, clothing and shelter, we seek forms of entertainment and relaxation like television, films, books and music, interaction and friendship with other human beings, travel and so on.

But that is not all. The soul, being spiritual and in some way unlimited, has a natural longing for what is beyond the material, for what is spiritual and even infinite. This is easy to see.

We distinguish two principal faculties of the soul: the intellect, or mind, and the will. The intellect by its nature seeks truth. All sorts of truth. We are naturally inquisitive. We want to know. When we come across a question that interests us, we want to know the answer. We see this in children, who are constantly asking questions: why is the sky blue, where do babies come from, how do fish breathe under water?

We adults want answers to all sorts of questions too. Less important ones like whether it is going to rain tomorrow when we are going on a picnic, whether the share market is going up or down, whether we are going to keep our job, whether our son is going to visit us, whether our team is going to win...

And really important questions, like where the universe came from and how it got started, why there are laws and harmony in nature instead of chaos, whether there is life after death... And whether there is a God. Since God is ultimately the answer to these deeper questions, we are really seeking God all along, whether we look at it that way or not.

In addition to our intellect, which by nature seeks truth, our soul has a will, the faculty by which we choose this or that course of action, and by which we love, desire, etc. The will by its nature seeks a good, or at least what is perceived to be a good. Even when we choose the wrong thing, it is because we saw something good in it.

When we find a good, we find happiness. That is in fact what happiness is: the emotion that follows upon the possession of a good. We seek and find happiness in lesser goods like a good meal, a good movie, a good trip, money in the bank and so on. But we also seek greater goods like friendship and other loving relationships. All of these give us varying degrees of happiness.

But so often, even when we have these goods, we find ourselves still lacking the happiness we desire. Some of the richest and most successful people, who seem to have everything, are very unhappy. The reason is that the will, like the intellect, is part of our spiritual soul which, being spiritual, is somehow unlimited. It will be fully satisfied only when it finds the ultimate good, the infinite good. That good is God himself.

We have no doubt seen this in talking with the many people we have known throughout our life. We find that some of the happiest ones are not the most successful, the most wealthy, but

34

rather people with a simple lifestyle, with a loving family, and who have God as very important in their life. Even when they may be suffering, they seem to have a certain joy about them. They are not troubled about what the future holds. They trust in God, who will look after them. And, in the end, they know that something much greater awaits them when they die – union with God in heaven. Perhaps, some will say, they are deluded – they put their trust in a God who doesn't exist. Maybe so. But maybe not.

What do we conclude from all this? That we human beings by our nature long for something beyond what satisfies us here on earth. We long for more, even though we may not know what it is. We long for answers to our deepest questions and we long for a happiness that is never complete in this life. And just as in animals, including ourselves, the longing or instinct stamped in their nature for such things as food, water, shelter, etc., is there because they need them for survival, so if we humans have a longing for something beyond us, it must be because the answer to that longing is to be found somewhere. This doesn't prove that there is life after death, but it points us in that direction. If we have these deep-seated tendencies, it must be because somewhere, somehow, sometime, there is something that will completely satisfy them.

That something can only be God, the infinite good, who is the origin of everything that exists. Only he can give us the truth and happiness we desire. But is there a God? That is our next question.

5

Is there a God?

In the first chapter we raised the question which everybody asks at some time or other: where did the world come from? Did it have a beginning or has it always been here? If it had a beginning, did it just spring into existence by itself, by chance, or did it have a creator? These questions are fundamental when we ponder the question of life after death. They lead us to the truth about the beginning of it all – and the end. So this is our first question: how did the universe begin?

The origin of the universe

Scientists are in substantial agreement that the universe has not always been here. It began to exist some 13.8 billion years ago, when the "big bang" occurred. And it has been expanding ever since. But maybe, you say, this was not the first "big bang". Maybe the universe is expanding at a decreasing rate because of the force of gravity, and soon it will reach its maximum extension. After that it will begin to collapse slowly and then faster until it all comes together in a huge mass, and then it will explode in another "big bang." And another. And another. And if that is the case, there may have been many "big bangs" before the present one. Maybe even infinitely many. Maybe.

But since the universe has now been shown to be expanding at an increasing rate, it is certain that before the "big bang" nothing existed. Nothing. But then how did the universe suddenly spring into existence out of nothing? It could not have begun by itself. Out of nothing, nothing comes. An outside force had to bring it into being. Who or what was that?

The well-known physicist Stephen Hawking, who occupied the professorial chair once held by Sir Isaac Newton at Cambridge University and who died in 2018, admitted in a television interview in 1989: "It is difficult to discuss the beginning of the universe without mentioning the concept of God. My work on the origin of the universe is on the borderline between science and religion, but I try to stay on the scientific side of the border. It is quite possible that God acts in ways that cannot be described by scientific laws."

In his popular book *A Brief History of Time* (1988), Hawking wrote: "Then we shall... be able to take part in the discussion of the question of why it is that we and the universe exist. If we find the answer to that, it would be the ultimate triumph of human reason – for then we would know the mind of God."

Just a moment, you say, you are quoting what Hawking wrote in *A Brief History of Time,* but you haven't mentioned what he wrote in his later book *The Grand Design*, co-authored with Leonard Mlodinow (Bantam 2010). Okay, let us see what he wrote there. In that book Hawking argued that God was not needed to create the universe. In a passage excerpted in the *Times* of London he wrote: "Because there is a law such as gravity, the Universe can and will create itself from nothing. Spontaneous creation is the reason there is something rather than nothing, why the Universe exists, why we exist. It is not necessary to invoke God to light the blue touch paper and set the Universe going."

Excuse me? Everyone knows intuitively that out of nothing,

nothing comes. It is simply not rational to say that out of nothing there suddenly sprang into existence the enormous amount of matter that gave rise to hundreds of billions of galaxies. As is to be expected, many of Hawking's fellow scientists ridiculed him on that point. Among them was Oxford Professor of Mathematics John C. Lennox. In his book *Gunning for God – Why the New Atheists are Missing the Target* (Lion Hudson 2011), Lennox showed the lack of logic in saying that the universe created itself: "If I say 'X creates X', I presuppose the existence of X in order to account for the existence of X. To presuppose the existence of the universe, to account for its existence, is logically incoherent. What this shows is that nonsense remains nonsense even when talked by world-famous scientists" (p. 32).

In a speech shortly before his death, Hawking said: "We are each free to believe what we want, and it's my view that the simplest explanation is that there is no God. No one created the universe and no one directs our fate. This leads me to a profound realisation: there is probably no heaven and afterlife either. I think belief in the afterlife is just wishful thinking. There is no reliable evidence for it, and it flies in the face of everything we know in science. I think that when we die, we return to dust. But there is a sense in which we live on, in our influence, and in the genes we pass to our children."

Stephen Hawking, like everyone else, was entitled to believe whatever he wanted. But now, in death, he knows whether there is life after death or not. Let us be clear about this. What happens after we die does not depend on what we personally think is going to happen. There is reality, truth, out there, just as there is reality here on earth. That is why I am writing this book, and why you are reading it. To discover the truth about what awaits us.

The very existence of the universe, which could not possibly have sprung into being by itself, is telling us there had to be some outside force to get it started. And that outside force had to be somehow of great, even infinite, power and intelligence. It could only have been God. But let us continue.

The Anthropic Principle

Over the years we have seen magnificent photos of galaxies, planets and stars taken by sophisticated telescopes. And there have been probes sent to explore other planets in the solar system. We have remained in awe at the vastness of the universe. Everywhere we see barren, hostile surfaces, freezing cold or exceedingly hot, incapable of supporting life. In striking contrast, we see our planet Earth, with its deep blue oceans, green rain forests, jungles, and all forms of life, including human life. How did this come about?

Before we go on, let me warn you that there is a little science and mathematics in what follows. Don't worry about that if this is not your area. Just skip over the technical bits and latch on to the conclusions that follow from them. That is what matters.

One of the extraordinary aspects of our planet is that it seems to be "fine-tuned" to support life, human life in particular. This has led scientists and philosophers to come up with what they call the "Anthropic Principle", from the Greek word for man, *anthropos*. According to the principle, there is a series of characteristics, or constants, in nature – the force of gravity or gravitational constant, the nuclear weak force constant, the nuclear strong force constant and the electromagnetic force – which are exactly what they need to be for the universe to support life. If they varied only slightly, life would be impossible.

For example, scientists tell us that if the gravitational constant or the nuclear weak force constant varied from their values by only one part in 10^{50} – that is one in 10 with 50 zeroes after it – then either the universe would have suffered a catastrophic collapse or it would have exploded throughout its expansion, both of which would have prevented the emergence and development of any form of life. This cannot be reasonably explained by pure chance.

And if the nuclear strong force constant were higher than its value by only 2%, there would be no hydrogen in the universe and therefore no water, both necessary for life. If, on the other hand, the nuclear strong force constant were 2% lower than its value, then no element heavier than hydrogen, such as helium, carbon, etc., could have emerged in the universe. This too would have made life impossible.

If the gravitational constant, electromagnetic force, or the proton mass relative to the electron mass varied from their values by only a tiny fraction (higher or lower), then all stars would be either blue giants or red dwarfs. These kinds of stars would not emit the proper kind of heat and light for a long enough period to allow for the emergence and development of life forms.

If the weak force constant had been slightly smaller or larger than it is, then supernovae explosions would never have occurred. If these explosions had not occurred, there would be no carbon, iron, or earth-like planets.

British astronomer Sir Frederic Hoyle (1915-2001) and American nuclear physicist and Nobel Prize winner William Fowler (1911-1995) discovered the exceedingly high improbability of oxygen, carbon, helium and beryllium having the precise qualities to allow for both carbon abundance and carbon bonding, necessary for life. This "anthropic coincidence" was so striking that it caused Hoyle to abandon his previous atheism and declare: "A common sense interpretation of the facts suggests that a super-intellect has monkeyed with physics, as well as with chemistry and biology, and that there are no blind forces worth speaking about in nature. The numbers one calculates from the facts seem to me so overwhelming as to put this conclusion almost beyond question" (*Annual Reviews of Astronomy and Astrophysics*, 20, 1982, p. 16).

Looking at more obvious facts, the distance of the earth from the sun is just right to support life. Any nearer and it would be too hot, any farther away and everything would freeze. A change of some two percent would mean the end of all life. Likewise, surface gravity and temperature have to be within a few per cent of what they are for the life-sustaining atmosphere to have the right mix of gases necessary for life. And the planet must rotate at just the right speed: too slow and the temperature differences between day and night would be too extreme; too fast and wind speeds would be very high.

The probability of all these forces and factors being, by chance, what they are is so small that some have compared them to a monkey randomly striking the keys of a word processor and producing the complete works of Shakespeare. You understand what I mean.

In their efforts to explain away the cause of this fine-tuning of the universe, some scientists have proposed the "multiverse" theory, according to which there are many, possibly infinitely many parallel universes, so that it is only natural to expect that in one of them there would be life. But there is simply no evidence for other universes and, in any case, they too would require fine-tuning in order to exist, let alone support life. Philosopher Richard Swinburne sums it up with a touch of humour: "To postulate a trillion-trillion other universes, rather than one God, in order to explain the orderliness of our universe, seems the height of irrationality." (*Is there a God?*, Oxford University Press, 1996, p. 68).

Order in the universe

If the fine-tuning of the universe to support life is so extraordinary, another "mystery" is the fine-tuning necessary for the universe to exist at all. American writer Eric Metaxas wrote in *The Wall St Journal* in 2014: "The fine-tuning necessary for life to exist on a planet is nothing compared with the fine-tuning required for the universe to exist at all. For example, astrophysicists now know that the values of the four fundamental forces – gravity, the electromagnetic force, and the 'strong' and 'weak' nuclear forces – were determined less than one millionth of a second after the big bang. Alter any one value and the universe could not exist.

"For instance, if the ratio between the nuclear strong force and the electromagnetic force had been off by the tiniest fraction of the tiniest fraction – by even one part in 100 quadrillion – then no stars could have ever formed at all. Feel free to gulp. Multiply that single parameter by all the other necessary conditions, and the odds against the universe existing are so heart-stoppingly astronomical that the notion that it all 'just happened' defies common sense. It would be like tossing a coin and having it come up heads 10 quintillion times in a row. Really?" (Reprinted in *The Australian*, 30 December 2014).

Also, if the universe were somehow the result of chance rather than of creation by an intelligent all-powerful being, we would expect it to be chaotic and unintelligible. But it has laws, such as the laws of physics and chemistry, that are universally valid and can be grasped by the human mind. This is a mystery that led Albert Einstein, arguably the greatest scientist of the twentieth century, to say: "The most incomprehensible thing about the universe is that it is comprehensible." He went on to say that he considered this comprehensibility "a miracle" or "an eternal mystery", since in principle one would expect a chaotic world which could not be grasped by the mind. What is more, this miracle "is being constantly reinforced as our knowledge expands." He went on to say: "My religion consists in a humble admiration of the superior unlimited spirit which is revealed in the minimal details which we are able to perceive with our fragile and weak minds. This conviction, deeply emotional, of the presence of a rational superior power which is revealed in the incomprehensible universe, forms my idea of God" (*Letters to Solovine*, New York, Philosophical Library, 1987, p. 131).

The origin of life

If what we have just seen is not enough, one of the greatest mysteries in the universe is how life first appeared. At the time of the "big bang", when everything was supposedly extremely hot, life was impossible. Yet some 3.5 billion years ago the first living organism suddenly appeared. How did this happen? Even the simplest living organism, like a bacterium, is exceedingly complex. How did it put itself together? Was it by the random collision of molecules?

In the early 1980s non-believers Sir Frederick Hoyle and mathematician Chandra Wickramasinghe set out to calculate the probability of the simplest living thing forming itself by chance in the "prehistoric soup", the atmosphere surrounding the earth. They knew it had to be composed of hundreds of thousands of proteins, each in turn composed of long chains of amino acids in exactly the right configuration to be able to live and reproduce itself. They came up with a probability of one in $10^{40,000}$, an infinitesimal probability, and they therefore concluded that life could not possibly have arisen by chance.

In evaluating this probability it is helpful to know that the total number of subatomic particles (electrons, protons, neutrons, quarks, leptons, etc.) in the universe is estimated to be about 10^{80} so that scientists consider anything with a probability of less than one in 10^{80} to be, for all intents and purposes, impossible. Yet the probability calculated by Hoyle and Wickramasinghe was many thousands of times less than that. Hoyle famously compared the probability of the spontaneous formation of life with the odds of a tornado blowing through a junkyard producing a 747 jet aircraft! (*The Intelligent Universe*, London, Michael Joseph, 1983, p. 19).

Okay, so life could not possibly have arisen by chance. But life is here. How did it begin? Hoyle was led to admit that life needed a creator, whom he called a "super-intellect", in outer space. This "super-intellect" supposedly created life somewhere out there and sent it to earth, where it suddenly appeared. "Super-intellect" is one way to explain it. Or one can use more conventional terminology and simply call this being "God". To this day, no one has come up with any other explanation for the origin of life.

One attempt to answer the question has come from Harvard University, which has poured millions of dollars into its Origins of Life Initiative, which began in 2005 with the collaboration of scientists in a wide variety of fields. Yet, after all this time and money, Dimitar Sasselov, Director of the Initiative and Professor of Astronomy, admitted in an interview with *Harvard Magazine* in September-October 2013, that the question of how life began on earth "is one of the big unsolved questions humanity has always asked."

One prominent atheist who was led by this mystery to believe in God was Oxford graduate and professor of philosophy Antony Flew. In an interview with BBC radio on 10 December 2004, he gave as a reason for his conversion to belief in God, after fifty years of professed atheism, that the study of DNA has shown, "by the almost unbelievable complexity of the arrangements which are needed to produce life, that intelligence must have been involved."

Order and purpose in nature

Everywhere we look in nature we see order and purpose. Plants take advantage of sunlight and water to grow, and to put out seeds that grow into other plants. Animals have instincts to warn them of dangers they have not seen before, to eat certain foods that are suitable for them and to avoid others that are harmful. They have an anatomy and a reproductive system that makes them male or female and they come together to produce offspring. The human body has a marvellous digestive system, immune system, circulatory system, respiratory system, reproductive system, etc., where all the parts work together so that the person can live and grow. How did this come about if the world was just the product of chance?

Or consider the order and purpose at the level of the individual cell. Microbiologist Michael Denton, in his book *Evolution, a Theory in Crisis,* says that the break between the non-living and the living world "represents the most dramatic and fundamental of all the discontinuities in nature. Between a living cell and the most highly ordered non-biological systems, such as a crystal or a snowflake, there is a chasm as vast and absolute as it is possible to conceive" (*Evolution – a Theory in Crisis*, Bethesda Maryland, Adler & Adler, 1986, pp. 249-50).

He describes the complexity of even the tiniest of bacterial cells, weighing less than a trillionth of a gram, as "a veritable microminiaturized factory containing thousands of exquisitely designed pieces of intricate molecular machinery, made up altogether of 100 thousand million atoms, far more complicated than any machine built by man and absolutely without parallel in the non-living world." (*ibid.* p. 250) What is more, the "factory" can reproduce its entire structure in a matter of hours.

Denton goes on to ask whether such a factory could possibly

have resulted from chance. "Is it really credible that random processes could have constructed a reality, the smallest element of which – a functional protein or gene – is complex beyond our own creative capacities, a reality which is the very antithesis of chance, which excels in every sense anything produced by the intelligence of man?" (*ibid.* p. 342).

Some of the greatest scientists in history have concluded that the cause of the incredible complexity, design and purpose in nature can be none other than God himself.

Sir Isaac Newton wrote in his *Opticks* in 1721, "How are the bodies of animals to be contrived with so much art, and for what ends were their natural parts? Was the eye contrived without skill in optics, and the ear without knowledge of sounds? ... Does it not appear from phenomena that there is a Being incorporeal, living, intelligent ...?"

Seventeenth-century German astronomer and mathematician Johannes Kepler wrote: "The chief aim of all investigations of the external world should be to discover the rational order which has been imposed on it by God, and which he revealed to us in the language of mathematics" (cited in J. Lennox, *God's Undertaker – Has Science Buried God?*, Oxford, Lion Hudson 2009, p. 21).

Wernher von Braun, the German aerospace and rocket engineer, went so far as to say: "I find it as difficult to understand a scientist who does not acknowledge the presence of a superior rationality behind the existence of the universe as it is to comprehend a theologian who would deny the advances of science" (cited in McIver, T. 1986, "Ancient Tales and Space-Age Myths of Creationist Evangelism", *The Skeptical Inquirer 10:258-276)*.

Paul Davies, British astrophysicist, writes: "There is for me powerful evidence that there is something going on behind it all... It seems as though somebody has fine-tuned nature's numbers to make the Universe....The impression of design is overwhelming" (*The Cosmic Blueprint: New Discoveries in Nature's Creative Ability To Order the Universe*, New York: Simon and Schuster 1988, p.203).

And Alan Sandage, winner of the 1991 Crafoord prize in astronomy, says: "I find it quite improbable that such order came out of chaos. There has to be some organising principle. God to me is a mystery but is the explanation for the miracle of existence, why there is something instead of nothing" (In Willford, J.N., "Sizing up the Cosmos: An Astronomers Quest", *New York Times*, March 12, 1991, p. B9).

The origin of man

If the origin of life and the ordered complexity of nature are mysteries that can only be explained by an intelligent designer and creator, the origin of man is yet another. How did a being with a spiritual soul, with rational intelligence, capable of thinking, planning and even wondering whether there is a God come into existence? Could it have evolved from the material life forms that came before it? We know that no ape or other living thing has rational intelligence. None of them can think, write books or symphonies, or in short, make progress in any way. They simply live in the same way they always have, following their instincts.

Man, on the contrary, clearly has rational intelligence – we can think, make progress in transportation, communication, medicine, construction, etc. To have rational intelligence, as we have seen, implies having a spiritual faculty, a spiritual soul. But spirit cannot evolve from matter. It is altogether different from matter. The only explanation for the existence of a spiritual soul is that man has received his soul from another being who is also spiritual. This being can only be the infinite pure spirit, God.

Oxford Professor of Mathematics John Lennox has commented somewhat humorously: "There are not many options – essentially just two. Either human intelligence ultimately owes its origin to mindless matter, or there is a Creator. It is strange that some people claim that it is their intelligence that leads them to prefer the first to the second" (*God's Undertaker – Has Science Buried God?*, p. 210).

In summary

In short, everywhere we look in nature we find evidence for an all-powerful, all-intelligent being who gave it its existence and its ordered design. Science has not only not done away with belief in God, but rather it has led to the certainty that there has to be a supreme intelligence behind it all. In the words of Lennox, "I submit that, far from science having buried God, not only do the results of science point towards his existence, but the scientific enterprise itself is validated by his existence" (*ibid.* p. 210).

In the face of all the evidence of science, it is not difficult to believe in God. It is more difficult not to believe in him. When all is said and done, an atheist needs more faith than a believer. Yes, you heard me correctly. A believer needs only enough faith to believe that it was God who created this vast universe with its harmony, order and purpose, who created life, and the human being... The atheist needs the faith to believe that somehow it all just happened by chance. What is more, the believer's faith is based on reason, on science, on the observation of the universe. The atheist's faith is blind, with no evidence to support it. On the contrary, all the evidence points to the existence of God.

Of course, you remain free to believe whatever you want. But one of these options makes much more sense than the other. John Lennox has summed it up on his website: "If religion is a fairytale of those afraid of the dark, then atheism is a fairytale of those afraid of the light."

It is this belief in God which answers the deeper question of the meaning and purpose of life. Life, and much later humans, did not spring into existence by the chance collision of molecules billions of years ago. If that were the case, life would have no meaning. We would be, as we suggested before, no more than a cork bobbing on the waves of the ocean, destined to sink and be seen no more. No, we too were created by an all-powerful, all-knowing and all-loving God who has given each of us a purpose in life, a reason to exist.

This moves us to ask: What can we know from reason alone about this God who created the universe out of nothing? We can know that he exists, but what sort of being is he? That is our next question.

6

What is God like?

When we ponder the question of how any being could have created out of nothing a universe with hundreds of billions of galaxies, we are left with our mouth open. It is simply humanly incomprehensible. And that this being is spiritual, with no body, also leaves us gasping. How can a being, someone, with no body, no matter, create so much matter? Again, from the human point of view, we find it impossible to comprehend.

The fact is that God, from the point of view of the human mind, is indeed incomprehensible. Our limited human capacity for understanding simply cannot get itself around the vastness of God. Nonetheless, there are some things we can know about God, even though we may not fully comprehend them. Let us consider a few.

First, there is *just one God*, not many. By the name God we mean the supreme, infinite being who created the universe. There cannot be more than one God for the simple reason that, if there were, each one would have something that the others did not, and therefore none of them would be infinite. And, in addition, we would have to ask the question, who created them? If one of them created the others, then this one would be God, but the others would be created beings, not God.

Second, God is *eternal*; he has no beginning and no end. He always was, and he always will be. He was not created but is rather the creator of everything else. Again, we find ourselves before a mysterious concept: a being who had no beginning, who always was. In fact, we mean by eternal that God does not exist in time, as if his existence goes back into the distant past and will continue into the distant future. He exists outside of time, in what we call eternity, where there is no change, no before and after. There is no succession of passing moments, there is only *now*, an eternal present.

Third, because of his eternity, God is *immutable*, incapable of change. To change is to acquire some aspect of being that was not present before, like a different position, size, degree of knowledge, etc. It is to gain or lose something. But God cannot acquire anything because he is infinitely perfect; he has every perfection. Living in the eternal now, he cannot change in any way.

Fourth, God is *uncreated*, he had no creator to give him existence. He did not create himself either. He simply is. He is his own existence. We can't get our head around this, because we are only finite, but we know that it is the case. All we can do is accept it, because it is the truth. God, as we have said, is incomprehensible for us.

Fifth, God is *pure spirit*. He has no body or matter, as we do. Again, matter, any matter, is always limited by its extension. But God is not limited, he is infinite. No material thing could possibly create a universe with hundreds of billions of galaxies. Only a spiritual one could. That too is a mystery.

Sixth, God is *almighty*, all powerful, omnipotent. He has to be to create the universe. When we say almighty, all powerful, we mean just that. Not very mighty, or very powerful. Not many times more powerful than any being on earth. No earthly being, no matter how powerful, could create the universe – and out of nothing. Only an infinitely powerful, almighty being, could do that. And we know that he has done it, because the universe is here, all around us. As we have seen, scientists tell us that before this universe came to be there was nothing, and now there is something, lots of it – a universe with hundreds of billions of galaxies. It came from God almighty.

Seventh, God is *omniscient*, all knowing. He knows everything. He knows all things because he created all things. He created this universe, and he gave it its laws of physics, chemistry, thermodynamics, etc. He knows the nature of everything, because he gave everything its nature. What scientists are only now gradually discovering after centuries of prodigious effort, God knew all along because he created it. Only a supremely intelligent being could have created the universe with all its laws, order, harmony and complexity. Only God could create something as complex as a cell, as DNA, as an eye, an ear, a brain, or a whole human body.

And, by the way, we can't resort to evolution to explain the order and purpose in nature as if things gradually evolved to become what they are. First of all, there wouldn't be any creation to evolve if it weren't for God, who created it.

And yes, there is a degree of evolution within species over long periods of time. Animals become faster and stronger, weaker ones die out and stronger ones live to produce offspring. But an eye doesn't gradually evolve until it can finally see. It has to give sight from the beginning or the animal would be blind and it would die. And the digestive and reproductive systems cannot gradually evolve until the animal can digest food and reproduce. These systems, and all the systems of the body, have to be complete from the beginning or the animal could not live.

With his omniscience, God knows every aspect of every being in the universe. And he knows the past, the present and the future.

Since he is in eternity, outside of time, he sees the whole of time at once, as if it were in the present. It is like a person in an airplane looking down on an army marching through the mountains, seeing everything at once, whereas the soldiers see only what it is immediately around them at any moment. And, of course, since God knows the future, he knows not only what we have done in the past and are doing now, but what we are going to do until the end of our life. Nothing is hidden from him.

Eighth, and, as it were, the summary of all this, God is *all perfect*. He has every perfection to an infinite degree. He is all-knowing, all-powerful, all-loving, and so on. Whatever perfection we humans can imagine, or strive to grow in, God already has. Or better, God already is. He is love, he is wisdom, he is power, he is perfection.

All of this we can know about God from reason alone, by observing the reality of nature around us and reasoning back to its cause. We can know this with certainty, even if there are many aspects of God's existence and nature which we find difficult to comprehend. We come back to the fact that the human mind can never fully comprehend God as he is in himself. He remains incomprehensible. St Augustine (354-430), the great theologian and philosopher, puts us at ease: "If you understand, it is not God" (*Sermon* 52:16).

All of this fills us with awe and reverence for so majestic a being as God. Indeed, all civilisations have had a belief in God along with some form of worship. Some have worshiped God in nature, in animals, or simply in the heavens. They have had some form of prayer and ritual, often with a priesthood, and many have offered sacrifices to God. In short, it is natural for man to know that, above and beyond the world we can see, there is a supreme being who is the cause of it all, and who is to be worshiped.

Apart from reason, another way that some people have come to know that there is a God and to experience his love is through what are known as near-death experiences. That is our next topic.

7

Near-death experiences

A common argument of those who don't believe in God, or in life after death, is simple: How do we know? No one has ever come back from the dead to tell us about it. The answer is equally simple: people have come back to tell us about it – in different ways.

One of these ways is what are known as near-death experiences (NDEs). Here a person has experienced severe trauma, often a cardiac arrest in which they may be clinically dead for a time, and they feel their soul leave the body and be transported into another realm of existence. We mentioned them when talking about the soul in Chapter 3, and about the young New Zealander Ian McCormack in Chapter 2, with his near-death experience in Mauritius.

There are many thousands of documented cases of NDEs and many books and articles have been written about them. Some of the books have been bestsellers. There are numerous accounts on the internet of people who relate what they experienced during them. NDEs are as real as the life experiences we all have. I personally have known at least four people who have had them. My doctor friends too say they have known people who have had them. NDEs are worthy of consideration and we can learn something from them.

Across the thousands of people who have had NDEs, there are some common elements. The first is the soul leaving the body and hovering above it, fully aware of what is happening below, even though the person is unconscious. The person later recounts details of what they saw in the efforts to resuscitate them. A second stage, experienced by many, involves the soul going through a tunnel towards a bright light, where they experience great love, peace and joy, which they recognise as heaven. Some in that state are aware of a divine being bathed in light, and many see loved ones who have preceded them in death.

Many describe seeing their whole life flash by in an instant, including the effect their actions have had on others, a phenomenon which has come to be called the life review. Some experience hell, and others a place of purification known as purgatory. On returning to their body, they often describe the experience as having been more alive than ever before, and they are spiritually transformed. They invariably change their life for the better. The experience convinces them that what we know as death is just a passing into another realm of existence. They lose their fear of dying and feel more joy in this life.

The description of these experiences is remarkably similar among all who have had them, no matter what prior religious belief the person may have had. They may have had a strong belief in some religion or absolutely none, they may have lived a good life or been a big sinner, been an adult or a young child. It doesn't make any difference. They all have similar experiences.

Studies by Dr Jeffrey Long

Among the people documenting these experiences is Dr Jeffrey Long, M.D., a radiation oncologist in Louisiana. He has been collecting accounts of near-death experiences from around the world since 1998 and has studied almost five thousand of them. He has written several books, including the *New York Times* bestseller *Evidence of the Afterlife*. He has a website, NDERF.com, where he relates his findings.

In an interview with Goop, the wellness and lifestyle company, and published on their website, he says he has found that in a little over forty percent of cases the person observed things that were distant from their physical body. For example, in one account the soul travelled to the hospital cafeteria where it saw and heard their family and others talking, and later reported the conversation accurately.

He has some fifteen accounts where two people simultaneously had an NDE. In one of them an engaged couple were driving to Canada when they had a bad traffic accident. They were holding hands and felt a great love for each other as they rose above the car. There they were met by four spiritual beings, two of whom took the woman and moved away with her toward a light. The other two gently took the man back to the car, which was burning below him. He recovered consciousness in the car and his fiancée was leaning on his shoulder, even though he knew she was already dead. He understood he had been with her in sharing a near-death experience in the initial phase of her death and passage into life beyond the grave.

Dr Long has found that the great majority of those experiencing an NDE, when given a choice, do not want to return to their body and to life on earth. According to 75 to 80 percent of them, the reason is that they feel very intense positive emotions in their near-death experience, indescribable happiness, more so than they ever knew on earth. They greatly enjoy this experience, which some call heaven, and they have a sense of familiarity as if they have been there before. They very much want to stay and not return to earth.

In his most recent survey of people with NDEs, Dr Long asked whether the person encountered any awareness that God, or a supreme being, either exists or does not exist. He was astounded to find that virtually all, with one exception out of hundreds, answered yes, that they encountered an awareness of God, or encountered him directly. What is more, they never described God as judgmental, angry or wrathful. Rather they found an overwhelmingly loving presence, which gave them a great sense of peace. They often experienced a unity, a oneness with God, and many had a conversation with him.

When asked whether they received any information regarding the purpose and meaning of life on earth, a common response was yes, that we are truly spiritual beings who have an earthly existence, but our real nature is called to something beyond this life. We are on earth to learn lessons on how to live, how to love and be united with others, in order to prepare ourselves for the next life, where we really belong and where we will have a loving existence and be truly happy.

Dr Long found that only around one per cent of NDEs, were negative, positively hellish and frightening. He says there are two ways that people experience this hellish state: either at a distance, as if the person is passing it and looking at it from the outside; or, about half the time, when they are actually in that state themselves. He says that for many of those who experience this hell, they are clear afterwards that they needed an experience like that to make them face some issues in their life, to change and become more loving to others on earth.

I have personally known such a person. After a massive stroke, he saw himself in the judgment before God and realised he was going to hell. He begged God to forgive him and he came back to earth, where he changed his life radically for the better.

Dr Long has found that those who experienced the hellish state say they actually chose it themselves. That is, they were not forced to be there but rather it was their own free choices that led them there. He says that because these persons were such dark, evil beings, their "heaven" was to be surrounded by others who were like them in doing evil.

Dr Long is convinced by his research that what we call the soul is clearly distinct from the body, and the brain. He says: "It's just that there's some other part of us that seems to be intimately related to our consciousness and who we are, and what we are, that's much more than our physical brain. And it's non-physical clearly. Some call it the soul, but the term to use is neither here nor there. Every shred of evidence from near-death experiences and a number of other related experiences all convincingly point to the conclusion that consciousness, that critical part of who we are, survives physical brain death."

Studies by Dr Raymond Moody

The first person to write extensively on near-death experiences was Dr Raymond A. Moody, a psychiatrist whose book *Life After Life* (1975) was a bestseller. In *The Light Beyond* (Rider, UK, 2005), a revised and updated sequel to that book, he adds some interesting observations.

At the time of writing, he was devoting his entire psychiatric practice to counselling patients who had had near-death experiences and he had interviewed more than a thousand of them. He says those who have an NDE have some or all of the following experiences: a sense of being dead, peace and painlessness even during a "painful" episode, bodily separation, entering a dark region or tunnel, rising rapidly into the heavens, meeting deceased friends and relatives who are bathed in light, encountering a Supreme Being, reviewing one's life, and feeling reluctance to return to the world of the living (pp. 7-16). He says the experience changes the person's life for the better, and he identifies eight aspects of these changes.

First, these persons no longer fear death, even if they have lived a good part of their life fearing it. They are convinced that what we know as death is merely a passing to another state of existence. Even those who have had a "hellish" NDE do not fear a hellish punishment. In their life review they realised that the being of light loves and cares for them, that he is not judgmental, but rather wants them to develop into better people. Instead of living in fear, they focus on becoming more loving people.

Second, they sense the importance of love and almost all say that love is now the most important thing in their life. They usually feel much more joy in this life and they are convinced that there is a purpose to this life, which is to learn to love one another.

Third, they have a sense of greater connection with all things, including the world of nature.

Fourth, they acquire a greater appreciation for learning and a new thirst for knowledge. This is not knowledge for knowledge's sake but rather knowledge that contributes to being a more whole, complete person.

Fifth, they have a new feeling of control, of responsibility for the course of their lives. Having had the life review, they are more sensitive to the immediate and long-term consequences of their actions.

Sixth, they have a greater sense of urgency, of the shortness and fragility of their lives. It helps them see that their life is precious, that it is the little things that count, that they have to live their life to the full.

Seventh, they have a new awareness of the spiritual side of

life. Many are led to study and accept the spiritual teachings of the great religious thinkers. Dr Moody says that even people who didn't believe in God before, come to believe in him after an NDE.

Eighth, they have difficulty in re-entering and adjusting to the real world. After experiencing a spiritual paradise, it would naturally be difficult to come back to the mundane world.

Dr Moody has interviewed many children who have had NDEs and he finds that their experiences are similar to those of adults. He concludes that the experiences of children give better evidence for life after death than those of older people. The reason is that older people have had more time to be influenced by their life's experiences and their religious beliefs, whereas children come with a certain freshness. He says that the most important aspect of children's NDEs is the glimpse of the "life beyond" and how it affects them for the rest of their lives, moving them to be happier and more hopeful than those around them.

Some people have objected that NDEs are simply the consequence of a mental illness or psychotic episode, not a look into the next life. Here Dr Moody, as a psychiatrist, is in an excellent position to answer the objections and he is adamant that there is no mental illness involved. He analyses each of the mental conditions that have been proposed and rejects them all: psychotic conditions like paranoia, hallucinations, delusions and schizophrenia, oxygen deprivation leading to delirium, etc. He goes into great detail in each case and sums it up saying that, whereas mental illness leads to unhappiness, despair, depression and hopelessness, an NDE is likely to lead to mental adjustment and well-being that makes the person better adjusted than before.

Dr Moody concludes, after well over thirty years of studying NDEs, that those who have these experiences do get a glimpse of the life beyond, a brief passage into a whole other state of reality.

If we had one of these near-death experiences ourselves we would be convinced of the reality of the separation of the soul from the body and the entry into another life. But since, hopefully – because it requires a traumatic event like a cardiac arrest and clinical death – we won't have that experience, we have to rely on the word of others. Let us examine a few particular testimonies.

Personal testimonies

An especially well-known and convincing NDE is that of a four-year-old boy named Colton Burpo from Nebraska, U.S.A., popularised in the book and later the film *Heaven is for Real.* While undergoing surgery for appendicitis in 2003, Colton appeared to have died, but meanwhile his soul left his body and went to heaven. He was later able to describe events he could not possibly have known about in life. For example, he told his mother that when he was in heaven he had met his sister. His mother said he didn't have a sister, but Colton insisted he had met her. The mother then remembered she had had a miscarriage and this girl was undoubtedly the one she had carried in her womb. He also spoke of meeting his great-grandfather, who had died thirty years before Colton was born. He was able to describe him accurately, even though he had never seen him in life.

Another well-known case is that of Dr Eben Alexander, a neurosurgeon who has taught at various universities, including Harvard Medical School. Dr Alexander is the author of the bestselling book, *Proof of Heaven: A Neurosurgeon's Journey into the Afterlife*, published in 2012. Over the years Dr Alexander had heard many stories from patients who had experienced cardiac arrest and had passed into a different world in which they saw beautiful landscapes, were reunited with deceased relatives, and even experienced God. He says he regarded these stories as pure fantasy, because if a person does not have a working brain, they cannot be conscious.

Then, on 10 November 2008 he himself had such an experience. While in an induced coma after suffering meningitis, he was taken into a state where he experienced what people call heaven, and where he encountered God. Before that experience he could not reconcile his knowledge of neuroscience with belief in God, heaven or even the soul as something different from the brain. The experience completely transformed him, and today he believes that true health can only be achieved when we acknowledge that God and the soul are real, and that death is not the end of our existence, but only the passage into a different form of life.

A third well-known near-death experience is that of Dr Gloria Polo, a Colombian orthodontist, who, at the age of 36 and the mother of two children, was struck by lightning in May 1995 while walking on the campus of the National University of Bogotá with her 23-year-old nephew. Her nephew was killed instantly and Gloria went into cardiac arrest, with her body badly burned, inside and out. Her lungs, liver and kidneys were all burned, and her ovaries had dried up to a point where the doctors said they looked like black raisins. They told her she would not be able to have any more children, yet the ovaries somehow recovered and a year and a half later she gave birth to a baby girl, whom she named Maria José. Her legs were so badly burned that the doctors said they would have to amputate them. Gloria begged God to save her legs and a few days later the circulation returned and the operation was not necessary. The doctors said they had never seen anything like it.

Although, as a Catholic, she had been attending Sunday Mass, she had not been to confession since she was thirteen, she was using an intrauterine device for contraception, she had had an abortion and had paid others to have them, and she lived a very materialistic, self-centered and ungodly life. What is more, she had told others that devils do not exist and even that God did not exist.

While her body lay on the operating table, she began to see devils coming after her and she found herself falling down a tunnel into hell, where there was a horrible smell and millions of people, young and old, screaming in pain and grinding their teeth. She describes it as a dreadful place of hatred. She knew that this was the punishment she deserved for her sinful life, and that she was condemned to hell by her own will. The worst pain, she said, was knowing that God loves us so much and we are not with him. She saw that the sins that condemned her most included aiding and participating in abortion, receiving holy communion in a state of grave sin, fortune-telling, and speaking ill of priests.

In that state, she also saw the great suffering of the souls in what is called purgatory, a state of purification after death before entry into heaven. Her father was there in the lower levels, having lived a sinful life before a big conversion eight years before he died. Her mother was also there but higher up. Then she passed through a beautiful tunnel of light to a place of great joy and peace where she was able to embrace her deceased relatives. She also experienced her own judgment, seeing her whole life played out as in a movie with all her actions, good and bad, and the consequences of them. She understood how God regards sexual immorality, abortion and methods of contraception that cause abortions, as well as how he looked on her materialism, her excessive concern for her clothing and appearance, and her lack of faith.

She was given a second chance in order to amend her ways and tell others what she had experienced. She has written her account in the book *Struck by Lightning: Death, Judgement and Conversion* (Michael Journal, 2009), and she has since travelled the world, telling her compelling story. The message she leaves with her audiences is simple: "We have a God who loves us so much but also respects our free will. It's a God who loves you with so much passion. His mercifulness is so big. He is constantly seeking people's love, like a beggar. He doesn't force anyone to love him. So it's up to the individual."

Still another person who has had a near-death experience is Jim Woodford, a Canadian successful businessman and commercial airline pilot. He has written his account in the book, *Heaven, an Unexpected Journey: One Man's Experience with Heaven, Angels, and the Afterlife* (2017). His story can also be found in several talks on YouTube, including one at https://www.youtube.com/ watch?v=RfcTAoPSJEA. It premiered in August 2021 and had received over a million views when I accessed it in November of that year. It exemplifies some of the key ideas of this book.

Although he was born into a religious family and married a woman who went to church, Jim was not practising any faith and described himself as an agnostic. His business interests brought him considerable wealth, which allowed him to own several cars, a large boat, properties and even an airplane. With all of this, he says, he would lie in bed at night and ask himself, "Is this all there is?" He thought the answer lay in buying more cars, so he would go out and buy them. But, he acknowledges, what he was searching for was far beyond the wealth of this world, even though he didn't know it at the time. It was the absence of God in his life that created this emptiness. He considered himself "a lost cause" when it came to God.

In 2009 he began to feel ill and became progressively paralysed. He was eventually diagnosed as having Guillain-Barré Syndrome. Treatment led to recovery of most of his movement but he was still in considerable pain, which was tempered to some extent by an experimental medication he was able to obtain from overseas. Then, on 21 April 2014, he drove to a block of land he was selling and parked his truck. He decided to take more of the medication, even though he knew it was well in excess of what was prescribed. It immediately brought about a sensation of tremendous heat, he had difficulty breathing and he realised he was dying. At that moment, he says, he saw the truth of the saying that there are no atheists in foxholes. He felt remorse that, in spite of his great wealth, he had never thanked the creator, "if he existed". Then, he says, from some place inside him where he had never been for a long time, came the three words: "God, forgive me." He collapsed, hit his head on the steering wheel and passed out.

Then began a near-death experience in which he first found himself outside the truck with no pain and overwhelmed with joy. He looked back and saw someone sleeping in his truck, slumped over the steering wheel, with blood pouring from his mouth and nose. On looking more closely he realised it was himself. He then rose upwards at great speed, and passed through a tunnel of light to a beautiful pastoral scene. To his left he saw a deep crevasse with shiny black walls, a red fire at the bottom and a stench of decay and of all things evil. It filled him with dread, especially when a large creature came out with its body on fire, a horrendous face and hatred in its eyes. From within it came the screams of souls crying out for mercy. Filled with fear he turned back towards the light and said something he had never prayed in his life: "God, help me."

The creature was still there, coming towards him and calling out his name. Jim was astonished and said to himself: "It knew me! What did I do to deserve this?" In a voice that he describes as between a growl and a whisper, the creature said: "Jim, we are here for you. Join us." Frightened, he turned towards the light. It swept over him towards the creature, which screeched and ran away.

Then Jim saw three very tall and beautiful angels coming toward him, giving him a feeling of peace, love and safety. The first one put his arm around him and pressed him to his chest, saying: "Fear not, James, for we are your constant friends". They bowed low to him and one said: "When we look at mankind, we see the spark of life of our master." Jim realised that one was his guardian angel, who was reading from a thin, tiny book, the book of Jim's life. He realised that all he had to show for his deeds in a life he had considered of incredible success was this tiny book. It made him determined to go back, if he could, and fill his life with good deeds.

Later he saw a particularly beautiful creature of light, surrounded by angels, and recognised that it was Jesus Christ. Jesus looked at him with intense love and Jim found himself "lost in the love of eternity." He says that Jesus knew him intimately and loved him deeply, as if he were the only one he had created. From that moment, Jim knew that whatever happened to him, he belonged to Jesus forever. He pleaded to be allowed to stay in heaven, which he had yearned for without knowing it all his life, but he was told he should go back to tell others of the wonders he had seen.

He woke up in the hospital eleven hours after he had been found, scaring the nurses, who had told his wife there was no hope of his recovery, with no brain activity and complete organ failure. The doctors had decided to keep him alive until his wife and children arrived to say goodbye and then they would switch off the life support. To their amazement, his blood pressure returned to normal and his organs began working again. Jim has since written his book and set about telling the world of his experience.

What can we conclude from all this? Given the common experience of thousands of people of all beliefs and of none, young and old, we have powerful evidence for the existence of a spiritual soul which is distinct from the body; of a review of our whole life and all our actions, with their consequences; of a state of heavenly bliss where the happiness is so great that souls do not want to return to life on earth; of a state of hatred and suffering for those who have not been sorry for their sins; of a state of purification of the soul before entry into heaven; and of the existence of a supreme being who loves us and wants us to be with him forever. Those who have had a near-death experience have had a foretaste of what awaits us after death. For the rest of us, we will have to die in order to experience it in all its reality.

In addition to the numerous testimonies of people who have had a glimpse of what awaits us after death through near-death experiences, there are also accounts of people who have actually died and have come back to earth and appeared to others. Let us look at a few.

8

Back from the dead

In the near-death experiences we have just considered, a person was clinically dead, with their soul separated from the body, and they came back to earth to tell us about it. We might say they "almost died". But there are also cases where a person has actually died and later appeared on earth in a way that made them clearly recognised by others.

In a few of these cases the person died, was buried and came back to life in their body. The most obvious of these is Jesus Christ, who died on a cross outside of Jerusalem two thousand years ago and then rose from the dead and appeared numerous times in his body over the next forty days before ascending into heaven. We will consider Jesus' story later. But in most of these other cases the person appeared not in their physical body but, as it were, in their spirit, but still clearly recognisable.

One who has appeared in this way numerous times over the centuries is Mary, the mother of Jesus Christ. Let us consider three of her apparitions, which had extraordinary consequences and left no doubt that she had actually come back from the next life.

Guadalupe, Mexico, 1531

The first of these was her apparition in Mexico in 1531. It was the early days of the Spanish colonisation of Mexico and the missionaries were having only limited success in encouraging the Aztecs to embrace the Christian faith. According to the tradition, on 9 December 1531 an early convert named Juan Diego was walking near Tepeyac Hill outside Mexico City, when he saw a beautiful young woman whom he recognised as Mary, the mother of Jesus. Speaking in his native language, Mary asked Juan Diego to have a shrine built there in her honour. Juan Diego approached the bishop, the Spanish Franciscan Fray Juan de Zumárraga, but the bishop was naturally sceptical and told Juan Diego to ask the woman for a sign.

Three days later, on 12 December, Juan Diego was hurrying past the hill to attend to his dying uncle when Mary once again appeared to him. He explained that he was in a hurry to look after his uncle but Mary put him at ease, saying that his uncle would be cured, as in fact he already was. Juan Diego then asked Mary for some sign that he could take to the bishop and she told him to go to the top of the hill, where he would find some flowers growing. He did as he was told, even though December was not the season for flowers and, what is more, normally nothing grew on the barren hilltop. To his surprise he found some beautiful flowers in full bloom. Mary helped him arrange the flowers in his cactus fibre cloak, or tilma, and he went off to give them to the bishop. When he arrived at the bishop's house and showed him the flowers, an image of Mary suddenly appeared on his tilma. The image is now on display in the Basilica of Our Lady of Guadalupe in Mexico City and it has a number of extraordinary features.

The first is the very preservation of the fabric itself. Normally a cactus fibre garment would deteriorate within some twenty to forty years, yet here the fabric is still intact after almost five hundred years. Another is the brightness of the image, which has remained virtually unchanged over all these years. Various scientific studies have shown that the image was not painted, for it contains no pigment known to man. What is more, the image repaired itself after an ammonia spill in 1791 that damaged it considerably. And an attempt to destroy the image completely by exploding a bomb on the altar immediately beneath it on 14 November 1921 left the image unharmed, even though a wrought iron crucifix on the altar was bent double.

Perhaps the most extraordinary feature came to light when the image was photographed and then magnified 2500 times. In the partially closed eyes of Mary on the rough fabric there appeared the reflection of all those present in front of Juan Diego when the image first appeared. They include the bishop, his entourage and a family, a total of thirteen people. Because of the miraculous origin of the image and the symbolism on it, eight million Aztecs were converted to the Catholic faith in the next seven years.

Fatima, Portugal, 1917

Another extraordinary apparition of Mary was at Fatima, Portugal, in 1917. She appeared there each month from May through October to three small children, aged 10, 9 and 7. In the July apparition Mary made a prophecy that was borne out several months later. She told the children that on October 13 she would work a miracle that would be seen by everyone.

On October 13 some 70,000 people trudged through the rain and mud in the hope of seeing the miracle. Although it had been raining steadily, suddenly the clouds parted and the sun appeared. It began to revolve, sending out rays of light of different colours that lit up the surroundings, and then it seemed to fall towards the earth. The people fell on their knees and begged God for mercy and, to their great relief, the sun returned to its place. All those present and even some in the surrounding villages saw the miracle. Sceptics reported seeing it and the anti-clerical newspapers in Lisbon wrote articles about it. The fulfilment of the prophecy in such a dramatic way can only be explained if Mary did in fact come back to earth to prophesy the miracle, which then came about.

That is not the only prediction Mary made in the July apparition that was later borne out. She also told the children: "This war [the First World War (1914-1918), then in progress] will end, but if men do not refrain from offending God, another and more terrible war will begin during the pontificate of Pius XI. When you see a night that is lit by a strange and unknown light you will know it is the sign God gives you that he is about to punish the world with war..." Here Mary made three more predictions.

First, there would be another terrible war which was, of course, the Second World War, which began in 1939.

Second, the war would be preceded by a "strange and unknown light". On the night of 25-26 January 1938, an exceedingly bright light, like the Aurora Borealis or Northern Lights, was seen over a large part of Western Europe, as far south as Spain and Portugal. It was so exceptional that newspapers reported it. An article in the *New York Times* on January 26 read: "The Aurora Borealis, rarely seen in Southern or Western Europe, spread fear in parts of Portugal and lower Austria tonight while thousands of Britons were brought running into the streets in wonderment. The ruddy glow led many to think half the city was ablaze... The lights were clearly seen in Italy, Spain and even Gibraltar... Portuguese villagers rushed in fright from their homes, fearing the end of the world."

The third prediction was that the war would begin during the reign of Pope Pius XI. In 1917, when Mary appeared at Fatima, the Pope was Benedict XV, who was to die in January 1922. The new Pope, chosen on February 6 that year, could have taken any name he wished, but in fact he chose the name Pius XI. While the Second World War began, strictly speaking, with Hitler's invasion of Poland on 1 September 1939, when the Pope was Pius XII, it could be said that it began when Hitler annexed Austria and made claims over parts of the Czech Republic in 1938, during the reign of Pius XI.

Zeitoun, Egypt, 1968

Lest you think that Mary has appeared only to Catholics, consider her apparitions in Zeitoun, a suburb of Cairo, Egypt, beginning in 1968, where she appeared and brought about healings in people of all faiths. The story began in 1918, when it is said that Mary appeared in a dream to Khalil Ibrahim, who owned several plots of land in Zeitoun, asking him to build a church there in her honour and telling him that a miracle would take place. The church of St Mary, a beautiful white Coptic Orthodox church with four small domes over the corners and one large one in the centre, was completed in 1924.

In 1968, when the apparitions began, Christians were being persecuted in Egypt, with their enemies painting crosses on their front doors to identify them. On the evening of 2 April 1968, a 31-year-old Muslim named Farouk Mohammed Atwa, who worked across the street from St Mary's, saw what he thought was a woman dressed in white standing on the main dome of the church. He feared she was about to jump to her death and called out to her not to do it. The woman appeared to float effortlessly over the sloping roof of the church toward its cross, with her head bowed and her hands folded in prayer. Atwa pointed her out to the people standing nearby and they too saw her. They called the police, who arrived quickly, by which time a crowd had gathered.

A week later, on April 9, the woman in light appeared again for only a few minutes. From then on the apparitions were more frequent, sometimes two or three times a week, gradually becoming less frequent until the last apparition in 1971. It became clear to all that the figure was indeed Mary, the mother of Christ. She never spoke, but all were convinced that it was she who was appearing.

Sometimes she would be visible for only a short time and others for hours at a time. She always appeared to be praying, sometimes bowing toward the cross or blessing those watching on the streets below, sometimes remaining stationary and other times gliding across the church roof. Occasionally there appeared around her what looked like doves of light.

Over the next few years many healings took place. The first one involved Farouk Atwa himself who, the day after the first apparition, went for a scheduled operation to amputate a finger which had developed gangrene, only to discover that the finger had inexplicably healed. Among the others, a blind Muslim was given back his sight and was able to see Mary in one of the apparitions; a girl who had suffered from polio from the age of six months was able to walk again without the aid of crutches; paralysed people were cured of their paralysis; a woman with breast cancer saw Mary beside her bed and the following day the cancer disappeared.

People were able to take photographs of the apparitions, and newspapers, including the *New York Times*, carried articles about them. The number of people who saw Mary grew greatly and on one occasion numbered nearly 250,000 of all faiths: Orthodox, Catholics, Jews and Muslims. Overall, millions of people saw Mary, making these the most widely viewed apparitions in history. Even the Egyptian President Gamal Abdel Nasser saw them, leading him to soften his stance against Christians.

The Egyptian government conducted an investigation and,

after not finding any human explanation for the apparitions or any evidence of a hoax, declared that "it has been considered an undeniable fact that the Blessed Virgin Mary has been appearing on Zeitoun Church in a clear and luminous body seen by all present in front of the church, whether Christian or Muslim." People saw the apparitions as bringing a message of peace and hope.

These apparitions can only be explained if there is a state of existence after this life from which people can return to earth.

Apparitions from purgatory

As we recall from the last chapter, when Gloria Polo had her near-death experience after being struck by lightning, she saw her father and mother, and many other souls in what is known as purgatory, the state of purification of souls before they enter heaven. Over the centuries, numerous souls in purgatory have appeared to people on earth.

One such apparition is related by St Margaret Mary Alacoque (1647-1690), a Catholic nun: "When I was praying before the Blessed Sacrament on the feast of Corpus Christi, a person enveloped in fire suddenly stood before me. From the pitiable state the soul was in, I knew it was in purgatory and I wept bitterly. This soul told me it was that of a Benedictine, who had once heard my confession and ordered me to go to Holy Communion. As a reward for this, God permitted him to ask me to help him in his sufferings. He asked me to apply to him all I should do or suffer for a period of three months... It would be difficult for me to describe what I had to endure during those three months. He never left me and seeing him, as it were on fire and in such terrible pain, I could do nothing but groan and weep almost incessantly..." After three months of her hard penances, the soul went to heaven.

In the twentieth century, well-known saints Padre Pio and Faustina Kowalska had visits from souls in purgatory. These few well-documented accounts, of the many hundreds in existence, again speak to us powerfully of life after death. We will see more of them later when we consider purgatory in greater depth.

Apparitions from the "other side"

Another phenomenon is the appearance of someone who has died to a friend or relative who clearly recognises him or her. One such case involves Gabrielle, the wife of a friend of mine, who died of a heart attack in January 2014 at the age of 64. In December 2016, Michael, a well-known television journalist friend of her family, and also a friend of mine, was in Mass in Sydney's St Mary's Cathedral when he suddenly saw Gabrielle. It should be said that, as an investigative journalist, Michael was always sceptical about the truth of anything or anyone he was investigating.

He describes what he saw in his book *A Sceptic's Search for Meaning*: "I have now had the most indescribable experience of seeing someone in heaven. I know that is a big statement and one which will be questioned by many. But my belief in the authenticity of this experience is unshakeable... It is an innocuous image of her that I see but, oh, so powerful: her full face, her hair and a hint of the top of her shoulders... I am stunned by how beautiful she is. She was a beautiful young woman when I first met her, but she was in her sixties when she died and her looks, as you'd expect, had changed. But there is not the slightest doubt in my mind that this is my friend, Gabrielle. She appears as if she is in her late twenties and her beauty is beyond what I had encountered in life: smiling quietly with a look of contentment and relaxation... I have trouble finding the words because the ones that come to mind, like 'beautiful', 'relaxed', and 'serene', don't seem sufficient. They are too common and overused. Then the right word comes to me in a jolt: 'heavenly'."

Michael, by the way, had been diagnosed with cancer of the throat two months before. He writes: "Looking at it now, I can wonder if this was a message related to my fate: Was she telling me I'll be joining her soon? Or that everything's going to be okay? That I'll be cured! But I don't ask myself those questions at the time. They seem to simply not matter. I just feel great comfort ... and joy." Michael died of his illness in March 2019.

Six weeks after Gabrielle appeared to Michael, her husband Ron rang Michael with the news that someone else had seen her. It was a lawyer from Melbourne, who was also a family friend. Unaware of Michael's experience, he wrote his own account: "On the evening of Saturday, 14 January 2017, I went to bed about 11.30 pm. A few hours later, 2.30 am, while still asleep, a young and very beautiful woman appeared to me. I thought she was aged in her twenties. I could only see her from the shoulders upwards. Her face was beautiful. She was happy, peaceful and heavenly. There was a certain luminosity about her face that was hard to describe... I only knew Gabrielle when she was about 60 years of age. I did not know what she looked like in her twenties, but somehow, I knew it was definitely Gabrielle. Immediately after the vision, I woke up. The whole thing was very real to me. When I woke, I could recall every detail and immediately woke my wife and told her what had happened."

At the time, this man had just been diagnosed with thyroid cancer, and he believed Gabrielle's appearance to him could be related to the diagnosis. In any case, it was "a great consolation" for him.

Another reasonably common phenomenon is the apparition to people who are dying of their deceased loved ones or of other heavenly beings. People working with the dying have given numerous accounts of people on their death bed suddenly talking to someone who is not visible in the room but whom the dying person recognises. This vision is often of a family member who has died some time before. In one such encounter a woman whose son had died two weeks earlier saw her son, who told her he was coming to take her with him. What was extraordinary was that, given the mother's weak condition, she had not been told of her son's death. This can only be explained if the son was still alive in another state after he died.

Sometimes it is not clear who it is that the person is seeing. The dying person, who has been asleep or unconscious, suddenly opens their eyes, looks up, smiles, and then closes their eyes and dies. I personally know two people who have done this just before dying.

Similarly, a university lecturer once told me that, when he was at the bedside of his dying mother, he saw his deceased father and brother beside her bed. In another instance, related by a friend, a young boy who was dying said he saw Jesus at the window.

There are numerous accounts like these. Again, they can only be explained by the reality of a state of life beyond the grave.

Moving forward

The accounts we have just considered, both of near-death experiences and of people who have died and appeared again on earth, tell us that there is a form of life in another state after death. What is more, they speak to us about very particular events and states which follow death: the separation of the soul from the body, the life review, heaven, purgatory and hell, and all of them in relationship with a loving God. But are these states real? If there were a trustworthy and comprehensive body of teaching somewhere that accepts all of these states and explains them in greater detail, it would merit further study. Fortunately, there is such a body of teaching – in Christianity.

But, you may say, I am not a Christian. That doesn't matter. But because Christianity has a well-developed, systematic body of teaching, formulated over the last two thousand years on the very questions we have been considering, it makes sense to study it. Moreover, since Christianity is the religion of almost a third of the world's population, it deserves to be taken seriously.

Christianity, of course, is the religion founded by Jesus Christ. Practically everyone has at least heard of Christ. But who is he? And are his teachings worthy of belief? That is our next question.

9

Jesus Christ

A t this point you might be thinking, I am not a Christian and I have no particular love for Jesus Christ. Fair enough. You don't need to accept Jesus as God, as Christians do, but you can at least study his life, since he is certainly one of the great moral teachers of history, along with such figures as Buddha and Mahatma Gandhi, among others. It makes sense, therefore, to learn something about his life and teaching, especially his teaching on life after death.

For Christians, of course, Christ is not simply one more moral teacher. He is God, who became man and lived on earth two thousand years ago. In this connection we can consider what Oxford Professor John Lennox said of the God whose existence we see in the orderliness of the universe:

> Now, if the ultimate reality behind the universe is a personal God, this has very far-reaching implications for the human search for truth, since it opens up new possibilities for knowing ultimate reality other than the (scientific) study of things. For persons communicate in a way that things do not. Persons can reveal themselves in speech and thereby communicate information about themselves that the most sophisticated scanner applied to their brains could not reveal. Being persons ourselves, we can get to know other persons. Therefore, the next logical question to ask is: If the Creator is personal, has he spoken directly, as

distinct from what we can learn of him indirectly through the structures of the universe? Has he revealed himself? For if there is a God, and he has spoken, then what he has said will be of utmost importance in our search for truth" (*God's Undertaker – Has Science Buried God?,* p. 209).

Indeed, if God has spoken, then we will be interested to know what he has said. Well, he has spoken. First of all, as we have seen, he has spoken powerfully and clearly through the creation he has left us, which we can perceive and understand through our God-given mind. In addition, he has spoken through Jesus Christ, who lived on this planet two thousand years ago.

Christians believe that Jesus Christ is not merely man but God, the eternal Son of God, who took flesh in a woman named Mary and dwelt on earth two thousand years ago. But is this really credible? Before we examine the claim that Jesus was God, we might ask if we can be certain that Jesus ever really existed. Some people have doubted it, so it would be good to examine the claim. It is obviously in the Bible that we have the most comprehensive information on the life of Christ. But there are also other historical writings that speak of him.

Historical references to Christ

Some of the earliest writings are from the first-century Jewish historian Flavius Josephus. Born in 37 AD, Josephus was a priest and a Pharisee who wrote four books towards the end of the first century. His most ambitious work, completed around the year 93, was *The Antiquities,* a history of the Jewish people from creation to his own time. In it he describes how a Jewish high priest named Ananias took advantage of the death of the Roman governor Festus – both of whom are mentioned in the Bible – to have the apostle James put to death: "He convened a meeting of the Sanhedrin and brought before them a man named James, the brother of Jesus, who was called the Christ, and certain others. He accused them of having transgressed the law and delivered them up to be stoned" (*The Antiquities* 20.200).

All the details in this account from a Jewish historian are consistent with what the Bible tells us. Indeed, James the Less was referred to as "the brother of the Lord" (*Matthew* 13:55) since he was a relative of Jesus. The historians Hegesippus (110-180 AD) and Eusebius (ca 264-339 AD) said that James was put to death by the Jews in the northern Spring of the year 62.

Another more extensive reference to Jesus by Josephus in *The Antiquities*, reads: "About this time there lived Jesus, a wise man, if indeed one ought to call him a man. For he was one who wrought surprising feats and was a teacher of such people as accept the truth gladly. He won over many Jews and many of the Greeks. He was the Christ. When Pilate, upon hearing him accused by men of the highest standing among us, had condemned him to be crucified, those who had in the first place come to love him did not give up their affection for him. On the third day he appeared to them restored to life, for the prophets of God had prophesied these and countless other marvellous things about him. And the tribe of Christians, so called after him, has still to this day not disappeared" (*The Antiquities* 18.63-64).

The authenticity of the text was questioned by some during the Enlightenment but today there is substantial agreement among Jewish and Christian scholars that it is authentic, although there may have been some interpolations added by copyists. For example, the statement "He was the Christ", the Messiah long awaited by the Jews, could very well have been added by Christians. Nonetheless, we have here a very complete reference to Jesus from a first-century non-biblical source. We should note too that Josephus makes reference here to Jesus' resurrection from the dead: "On the third day he appeared to them restored to life".

Another exceedingly important text is that of the Roman historian Tacitus (ca 55-120 AD). In his *Annals,* written in 115 AD, he describes how Nero persecuted the Christians in order to divert suspicion from himself for the fire that destroyed Rome in the year 64: "Nero fastened the guilt and inflicted the most exquisite tortures on a class hated for their abominations, called Christians by the populace. Christus, from whom the name had its origin, suffered the extreme penalty during the reign of Tiberius at the hands of one of our procurators, Pontius Pilatus, and a most mischievous superstition, thus checked for the moment, again broke out not only in Judaea, the first source of the evil, but even in Rome" (*Annals* 15.44). Here again we have a clear and unquestionable reference to Christ and his death, from the most important Roman historian of that period.

Still another significant early text from a Roman historian comes from Pliny the Younger, the Roman governor of Bithynia, in modern-day in Turkey. Pliny was the nephew of Pliny the Elder, the encyclopedist who died in the eruption of Vesuvius in the year 79. In a letter to the emperor Trajan around the year 111, seeking advice as to whether his way of dealing with Christians was correct, he said that Christians "also declared that the sum total of their guilt or error amounted to no more than this: they met regularly before dawn on a fixed day to chant verses alternately amongst themselves in honour of Christ as if to a god, and also to bind themselves by oath, not for any criminal purpose, but to abstain from theft, robbery, and adultery" (*Letters*, 10.96).

On the basis of these texts, among others, there can be no question about Jesus' actual historical existence. But who was this Jesus?

Jesus Christ, God and man

As most people know, including non-Christians, Jesus Christ was a religious leader who lived in Israel in the first decades of the first century AD. The whole world uses a calendar which numbers the years from Christ's presumed birth in the year 1. It is interesting to note, nonetheless, that because Jesus was born during the reign of King Herod the Great, who died in 4 BC, Jesus was born sometime before the year 1.

The Bible tells us that Jesus was born of a virgin mother named Mary, who was betrothed at the time to a man named Joseph. As the gospel of Luke relates, an angel sent by God appeared to Mary in the home of her parents in Nazareth, in Galilee in the north of Israel, and announced that she was to be the mother of the long-awaited Messiah, the Christ, or anointed one. Moreover, the angel told her that her son would be the very son of God.

The Jewish people had been awaiting the Messiah for centuries. It is clear in the Old Testament Jewish scriptures that a Messiah would come who would be a descendant of the great King David, who would be a prophet like Moses, who would deliver the people of Israel from their oppressors and who would usher in an age of peace. More specifically he would come from the tribe of Judah, he would be born in the town of Bethlehem, where David had been born, and he would be born of a virgin. All of these prophecies were fulfilled by Jesus.

Christ lived for only some thirty-three years, the first thirty of which were spent working with Joseph, his legal father, in his workshop in Nazareth. Then he began the three years of his public life, in which he chose twelve men, whom he called apostles, to follow him closely and carry on his mission after he died.

During those three years, Christ travelled throughout Israel, teaching the people the way to a better life and preparing them for the life with him in heaven to which he was calling them. He worked many miracles, curing the sick, healing lepers and a man who was blind from birth, multiplying a handful of bread and fish to feed thousands of people, calming storms and raising three people from the dead. He was constantly followed by great crowds of people, who hung on his every word and brought him their sick loved ones to be healed.

At the same time he was forming the apostles to be the leaders of the Church he founded, placing the apostle Peter at the head. As he neared the end of his short life, he began to warn the apostles that he would have to suffer and be put to death by crucifixion, but he would rise from the dead on the third day.

In fact, the leaders of the Jews saw Christ as a threat to their power, since he was drawing many people away from them. What is more, Christ claimed to be God and, for the leaders of the Jews, this was blasphemy. No man could be God, so they plotted to have him put to death. This they succeeded in doing by telling the Roman governor, Pontius Pilate, that Jesus was setting himself in opposition to the Roman emperor, supposedly by forbidding the payment of tribute to Caesar. Pilate, although personally convinced of Jesus' innocence, under severe pressure from the leaders and with the threat of a riot, ordered Jesus to be scourged and crucified.

On a Friday at the time of the Jewish feast of Passover, Christ was crucified on a hill named Calvary outside Jerusalem, between two thieves who were crucified with him. After three hours on the cross he died and his body was laid in a nearby tomb. Then, as he had foretold, he rose from the dead two days later on Sunday, a day which Christians celebrate as Easter. Over the next forty days, Christ appeared numerous times to his disciples. Finally, having given the apostles the mission to go out to all nations and teach the people what he had taught them, he ascended into heaven before their eyes.

The apostles first went back to Jerusalem where they prayed for the next ten days until, on the Jewish feast of Pentecost, the Holy Spirit, the Spirit of God, came down and filled them with boldness to preach the faith of Christ to the many people gathered in Jerusalem for the feast. Three thousand people were converted to the Christian faith on that day and a few days later the number had risen to five thousand.

After that, the apostles and other followers of Christ went out to many nations and the Christian faith gradually spread all over the Mediterranean region. Peter was put to death in Rome by the emperor Nero around the year 65 AD, and for the next 250 years the Romans persecuted Christians for not worshipping the Roman gods and goddesses, nor the emperor. In the year 313 the emperor Constantine issued the Edict of Milan, by which Christianity was given legal status in Roman law and should no longer be persecuted. And in 380, under the emperor Theodosius, the Roman senate proclaimed Christianity the official religion of the Roman Empire. In the following centuries, the Christian faith spread all over the world.

It is clear from this short history that Jesus was a remarkable person, whose teachings and Church took root all over the world. But if we are to believe what he said about life after death we would want to be convinced that he was truly sent by God. Or ideally, if that were the case, that he actually was God.

Was Jesus Christ God?

As we saw before, the angel had told Jesus' mother Mary that the son she was to bear would be the very son of God. St Luke records the angel's words: "He will be great and will be called the Son of the Most High; and the Lord God will give to him the throne of his father David, and he will reign over the house of Jacob for ever;

and of his kingdom there will be no end" (*Luke* 1:32-33). The Son of the Most High God is clearly God himself, and a kingdom that lasts forever is no earthly kingdom, but one in which God himself reigns. Later the angel told Mary that "the child to be born will be called holy, the Son of God" (*Luke* 1:35). In other words, it was clear from the angel's words that the child to be born of Mary would be God, the Son of God.

But did Jesus do anything that showed he was God? Yes, he did, both in what he said about himself and in what he did.

As regards his words, he made the distinction between the apostles' relationship with God the Father and his own. For example, after his resurrection when he appeared to one of his followers, Mary Magdalene, he told her to "go to my brethren and say to them, I am ascending to my Father and your Father, to my God and your God" (*John* 20:17). Jesus knew that he was the eternal Son of the Father while the apostles and other disciples were in a sense adopted sons, so that there was an essential difference between them. Jesus never spoke of "our Father" when including both himself and his followers. It was always "my Father and your Father".

On another occasion, when Jesus asked the apostles, "But who do you say that I am?", Peter answered, "You are the Christ, the Son of the living God" (*Matthew* 16:16). Peter had answered correctly, so Jesus told him: "Blessed are you, Simon Bar-Jona! For flesh and blood has not revealed this to you, but my Father who is in heaven" (*Matthew* 16:17). That is, what Peter could not know by human means, that Jesus was the very son of God, he knew because the Father in heaven had revealed it to him.

Moreover, Jesus knew that he was not just one more son of God like the apostles. He was the eternal Son who shared the Father's divine nature. He affirmed this when he said in the temple of

Jerusalem, "I and the Father are one" (*John* 10:30). Because this meant that Jesus was claiming to be God, the Jews took up stones to put him to death, saying: "We stone you for no good work but for blasphemy; because you, being a man, make yourself God" (*John* 10:33).

He went on to tell the Jews that if they did not believe him, they should at least believe his works, or miracles, "that you may know and understand that the Father is in me and I am in the Father" (*John* 10:38). Again, he is claiming to be God, one with the Father.

On the night before he was crucified, he prayed to his Father God: "And now, Father, glorify me in your own presence with the glory which I had with you before the world was made" (*John* 17:5). By these extraordinary words, he was claiming to have been with his Father God in the glory of heaven before the world was made; that is, from all eternity.

Later that night Jesus was arrested. The following morning he appeared before the Jewish high priest, who asked him: "Are you the Christ, the Son of the Blessed?" Jesus replied, "I am; and you will see the Son of man sitting at the right hand of Power, and coming with the clouds of heaven." To the Jews, it was blasphemy that anyone would claim to be the son of God, or to be seated at the right hand of God in heaven. In view of this the high priest said to those with him, "'You have heard his blasphemy. What is your decision?' And they all condemned him as deserving of death" (*Mark* 14:61-64).

It is clear from this that, by his words, Jesus was claiming to be God. He was either deluded, or he was God. The real proof that Jesus was truly God came in his works, his miracles.

As we have said, Jesus did many miracles during his three years of public life on earth. He healed the sick, cast out devils, calmed storms, restored sight to a man born blind, and especially he raised three people from the dead. His miracles explain, in good measure, why so many people followed him and became his disciples.

His greatest miracle, of course, was rising from the dead on the third day after his crucifixion, as he had foretold. He began by telling the apostles a long time beforehand how he was to die: "Behold we are going up to Jerusalem; and the Son of man will be delivered to the chief priests and scribes, and they will condemn him to death, and deliver him to the Gentiles to be mocked and scourged and crucified, and he will be raised on the third day" (*Matthew* 20:18-19).

All this came to pass. Moreover, it is certain that Christ actually died on the cross. John, who was there, records that the soldiers came to break the legs of the two men who had been crucified with him, but "when they came to Jesus and saw that he was already dead, they did not break his legs" but "pierced his side with a spear, and at once there came out blood and water" (*John* 19:32-34). Even the Roman historian Tacitus says that "Christ was put to death by Pontius Pilate, the procurator of Judaea, in the reign of Tiberius" (*Annals*, 15. 44).

Then on the third day, Sunday, the tomb where Christ was laid on Friday was found to be empty. All four gospels tell us this. During that day Christ appeared first to some women who had gone to the tomb to anoint his body, later to two disciples who had left Jerusalem for a nearby town called Emmaus, at some point to Peter, and finally that night to all the apostles gathered together. On this last occasion he said: "See my hands and my feet, that it is I myself; handle me, and see; for a spirit has not flesh and bones as you see that I have," and he went on to eat a piece of broiled fish before them (*Luke* 24:39, 43). He had truly risen in the flesh.

After that the apostles, filled with joy, began to preach that Christ had risen from the dead. No one would have believed them if it could be shown that Christ's body was still lying in a tomb just outside Jerusalem. The resurrection of Christ completely transformed the apostles. From frightened, disheartened men they were transformed into bold preachers of the resurrection. There is no way to explain this sudden change except by attributing it to the reality of the resurrection.

What is more, nowhere does anyone claim to have found the mortal remains of Jesus. We know where the remains of most of the apostles are, yet there is no claim anywhere to have the remains of Christ.

Finally, the very origin and survival of the Church argue powerfully in favour of Christ's resurrection and divinity. In the Acts of the Apostles we read how Gamaliel, a respected Jewish elder and teacher of the law, reminded the members of the Jewish council that a certain Theudas had about four hundred followers, but he was slain and his followers were dispersed. After him a Galilean named Judas had a number of followers, but he too died and his followers were scattered (cf. *Acts* 5:34-37). This would certainly have happened to the followers of Jesus too if he had not risen from the dead. Within a short time, the apostles would have dispersed and gone back to their work and ordinary life. As it was, they went all over the known world and preached the resurrection of Christ, most of them being put to death for doing so. Their preaching brought thousands of followers and the Church spread quickly throughout the Mediterranean world.

In summary, it is clear that Jesus Christ was truly God, and so we can believe what he said, including about life after death. But where do we go to find this teaching? Christianity derives much of its belief system from the Bible, which is a collection of writings comprising two main parts: the Old Testament, made up of Jewish writings prior to Jesus Christ, and the New Testament, with writings on Christ's life and teaching. But can we trust the

Bible? Were those who wrote those texts trustworthy? How do we know that the Bible texts we have today are faithful to the original ones written two thousand years ago? That is our next question.

10

The Bible

The Bible is undoubtedly the greatest bestseller of all time. It has gone through more editions, in a host of languages, and more copies printed than any other book. It is regarded by Christians as the very word of God, in the sense that it was God himself who inspired the various writers to put in writing what he wanted written.

It is especially in the New Testament, comprising the twenty-seven books written after the time of Christ, that we find the most comprehensive answers to the question of life after death. All of the New Testament texts were written by the close of the first century, no more than some seventy years after the death of Christ. But who wrote those books and are they trustworthy?

The writers of the New Testament

The first four books, called the gospels, relate the life and teachings of Christ. They were written by Matthew, Mark, Luke and John. Matthew and John were two of Christ's closest followers, or apostles. They were with him for the three years in which he travelled throughout Israel, preparing the apostles to lead the Church that would continue his mission after he died. They saw and heard what Christ did and said over that time and they wrote it down faithfully.

Mark and Luke were not apostles, but they were close followers of Peter and Paul respectively, both of whom were called by Christ for their mission. Peter, an apostle, was named head of the Church by Christ. Mark spent much time in the company of Peter and later wrote down what Peter had said in his teaching.

Luke was a follower of Paul, travelling with him and later writing down much of what he said. In addition to his gospel, Luke also wrote a book called the Acts of the Apostles, which relates the life of the early Church after the death of Christ.

Who was Paul? He was a Jew who had persecuted the followers of Christ and then had a dramatic conversion on his way to Damascus to arrest Christians. After that he became a staunch defender and preacher of Christianity and he went as far as Rome and possibly Spain, passing on the teachings of Christ. He wrote thirteen letters, which make up a good part of the New Testament. Another letter, to the Hebrews, bears the stamp of Paul's style, but it is not certain that he wrote it.

In addition to his gospel, John also wrote the last book of the New Testament, the book of Revelation, and three letters. Peter wrote two letters.

Two other letters were written by the apostles James and Jude.

All of these New Testament writings were accepted as genuine by the early Church, which used them in their prayer and worship, and they made copies to be sent to other communities.

The writers of these texts were completely trustworthy. They lived holy lives and suffered persecution for being followers of Christ. They had everything to lose and nothing to gain by defending the teachings of Christ. With the exception of John, who was banished to the island of Patmos but not killed, all the other writers of the New Testament were put to death for the faith they professed in Christ. There can be no doubt that what they wrote was a faithful reflection of what Christ said and did, as they were prepared to die for what they wrote and believed.

The trustworthiness of the Bible texts

But are the texts which we have in a modern-day Bible a faithful rendering of the originals, which of course are no longer in existence? We are naturally inclined to accept that they are. Of course, if we don't have the originals, we cannot be absolutely certain that our texts match them perfectly, but that is the case with all ancient writings. In the case of the New Testament, we are on very solid ground, much more so than with practically any other ancient writing.

When a document was written thousands of years ago, it was copied successively many times, and all this was done, of course, by hand. It is only natural that when copies are made of other copies, errors can creep in. But when the extant copies are numerous, and they come from widely differing geographical regions, and moreover they date back to a time close to when the original was written, we can be more confident that they are a faithful copy of the original. That is the case with the New Testament.

Added to this, when there are translations of the original documents which were made relatively early on, the translations can be compared with each other and so it is possible to work back to the original, even if there are no extant copies in the original language. In the case of the New Testament, practically all of which was written in Greek, in addition to numerous Greek manuscripts we also have early translations in such languages as Latin, Syriac and Coptic. Then secondary translations were made from these in languages like Armenian, Gothic, Georgian and Ethiopic.

But that is not all. In the case of the New Testament, even if we didn't have any of these manuscripts, there are still numerous quotations of New Testament writings in the many commentaries on Scripture, sermons, letters and other writings of the early Church saints and other writers, so that we could reproduce a great part of the New Testament just from them. When all of these writings are compared with each other, it is possible to establish with great accuracy the original text.

If we look at other ancient writings, we see how fortunate we are with the New Testament. For example, of the Roman historian Tacitus' *Annals of Imperial Rome*, written around 115 AD, there is only one extant manuscript of the first six books and it dates to around 850 AD. Of books eleven to sixteen there is another manuscript dating from the eleventh century, while books seven to ten are lost altogether.

And of Josephus' *The Jewish War*, written around 75 AD in Aramaic or Hebrew, there are only nine Greek manuscripts in existence, dating from the tenth, eleventh and twelfth centuries, plus a Latin translation from the fourth century.

By comparison, we have over 5000 manuscripts of the New Testament in Greek alone. The earliest of these were written on papyrus, which grew in the Nile delta in Egypt. The most significant are the Chester Beatty Biblical Papyri, which were discovered in 1930 and date back to the beginning of the third century. They contain portions of the four gospels, the Acts of the Apostles, the letters of St Paul, the letter to the Hebrews and the book of Revelation. Moreover, there are other papyrus manuscripts which date back to the beginning of the third century.

The very earliest fragment of a papyrus manuscript, containing five verses of chapter eighteen of John's gospel, is dated between

100 and 150 AD, judging from the style of the script. Considering that the gospel itself was probably written towards the end of the first century in the city of Ephesus in Asia Minor, the fragment is a very early copy indeed. And it was made in Egypt, a long way from where the gospel itself was written.

As regards the number of extant manuscripts of other ancient works, next after the New Testament comes Homer's *Iliad*, of which there are fewer than 650 manuscripts, some of them quite fragmentary. The work was written around 800 BC and the earliest partial manuscripts are from the second and third centuries AD, a long time after the original was written. The earliest complete manuscript is from the tenth century AD.

So we are on very solid ground in knowing the original text of the New Testament.

Archaeological evidence for the New Testament

What is more, recent archaeological investigations in Israel bear out the truth of some statements in the New Testament that had been contested by scholars. If there is archaeological or other scientific or historical evidence which contradicts statements in the New Testament, or the Old Testament for that matter, we would be inclined to doubt the truthfulness of the Bible. But if these findings consistently confirm what the Bible says, they confirm the credibility of the biblical text. There are a number of biblical statements which have been challenged by critics, only to be confirmed later by archaeological discoveries. A good source for this is Lee Strobel's excellent book *The Case for Christ* (Zondervan, Grand Rapids 2016).

For example, Luke says in the second chapter of his gospel that when Jesus was born, Joseph and Mary went to Bethlehem because the census decreed by Caesar Augustus required all to go to their own city. It has been questioned whether there was any evidence for a census around that time which made this demand. In fact, an official government census order from a Roman Prefect of Egypt dated AD 104 has been found which states that "it is necessary to compel all those who for any cause whatsoever are residing out of their provinces to return to their own homes, that they may both carry out the regular order of the census and may also attend diligently to the cultivation of their allotments."

Likewise, Luke says that the census was conducted when Quirinius was governor of Syria during the reign of King Herod the Great (cf. *Luke* 1:5, 2:2). But Herod died in 4 BC and Quirinius began to rule Syria in 6 AD. An archaeologist has recently found writing on coins which state that Quirinius was a ruler in Syria and Cilicia from 11 BC until after Herod's death. It seems there were two officials named Quirinius and the census Luke describes took place at the time of the first one.

Although this finding has been disputed by some, Sir William Ramsay (1851-1939), archaeologist and professor at Oxford and Aberdeen Universities, believed that Quirinius was a ruler in Syria on two separate occasions, one of which was during the time of an earlier census dated around 8-7 BC. Harold Hoehner, who earned his doctorate at Cambridge, says that Herod was ill and came into conflict with the emperor Augustus in 8-7 BC, so that it would have been reasonable for Augustus to order a census to assess the situation before Herod died.

Another controverted statement of Luke is in the third chapter of his gospel, where he says that Lysanias was tetrarch of Abilene when Christ was born. Some scholars have challenged this, saying that Lysanias was not a tetrarch but rather ruler of Chalcis some fifty years earlier. A tetrarch, by the way, is one of four joint rulers at a given time. But an inscription was found from the time of Tiberius, who was emperor from 14 to 37 AD, which names Lysanias as tetrarch in Abila near Damascus at the time Christ was born, confirming what Luke wrote. In fact, there were two officials named Lysanias.

Another example is Luke's use of the term *politarchs* for city officials in Thessalonica in Acts 17:6. Many historians have said there was no evidence for that term being used in any ancient Roman documents. Yet an inscription was found on a first-century arch, which reads, "In the time of the *politarchs...*", confirming the use of the term at the time of Luke. Archaeologists have since found more than thirty-five inscriptions that use the term, several of them in Thessalonica itself, dating from the time at which Luke was writing.

One prominent archaeologist examined carefully Luke's references to thirty-two countries, fifty-four cities and nine islands and found not one mistake on the part of Luke. The inference may be drawn that if Luke was so meticulous about geographical and other historical matters, he would have been equally meticulous and accurate in reporting events in the life of Jesus and the apostles.

Similarly, John in the fifth chapter of his gospel speaks of Jesus healing an invalid by the Pool of Bethesda with its five porticoes. Scholars have questioned this statement since no such place had ever been found in Jerusalem. But, following excavations which began late in the nineteenth century, the pool was found some thirteen metres beneath the ground, and indeed it had five porticoes or porches lined with columns.

Other archaeological discoveries that confirm John's writings are the Pool of Siloam (cf. *John* 9:7), Jacob's well (*John* 4:12) and the Stone Pavement near the Jaffa Gate where Jesus appeared before Pilate (*John* 19:13).

As regards Mark, Michael Martin, an atheist, accuses him of

being ignorant of the geography of Palestine since Mark says that "Jesus left the vicinity of Tyre and went through Sidon, down to the Sea of Galilee and into the region of the Decapolis" (*Mark* 7:31). Martin alleges that, given these directions, Jesus would have been travelling away from the Sea of Galilee, not towards it. But a study of ancient maps, with the probable roads between these places through mountainous terrain, reveals that Mark was correct.

The very existence of the town of Nazareth is another fact mentioned by the New Testament but questioned by historians, who say there is no mention of the town in the Old Testament, in other ancient Jewish writings or by any historian or geographer before the beginning of the fourth century. In 2006 the Nazareth Archaeological Project began excavating beneath the Sisters of Nazareth convent, a location known since 1880, and they found the remains of a first-century house, which conformed to the plan of a so-called courtyard house, typical of early Roman-period settlements in Galilee. Archaeologists found doors and windows, cooking pots and a spindle used in spinning thread. The presence of limestone vessels, which Jews believed could not become impure, suggests that a Jewish family lived there. Another first-century house was discovered nearby in 2009, all of which confirms the presence of a small Jewish town on the site of Nazareth.

So once again, we have external proof for many statements in the New Testament. In summary, we can trust what the Bible says. The New Testament is one of the most studied and authenticated of all ancient documents, especially in view of the extraordinarily large number of manuscripts from the earliest centuries still in existence.

As we have seen, it is in the New Testament that we find the most comprehensive record of what Jesus Christ said and did, including his teaching on life after death, which we will study in detail later. But it can sometimes be difficult to interpret and understand certain passages of the Bible. Different people may understand the same passage in quite different ways. How are we to know what the passage really means?

To find the most authentic interpretation of this teaching, we do well to have recourse to a Church which, apart from being by far the largest Christian denomination, traces its origin in an unbroken line back to Christ himself and has been interpreting and explaining the Scriptures for two thousand years: the Catholic Church.

11

The Church

To understand why we should look to the Catholic Church for the most complete teaching on life after death, as well as on other matters, we can take a brief look at the history of the Church and its claim to have the fulness of Christ's teaching. Again, you do not need to become a Christian, let alone a Catholic, but what we are about to study will help you see how it is eminently reasonable to listen to the teachings of this Church. They encapsulate all the teachings of Jesus Christ and, in particular, they explain in detail his teaching on life after death, which coincides with what thousands of people have described in their near-death experiences.

In the first few centuries after Christ, there was just one Christian Church. The Acts of the Apostles, in the New Testament, relate how the Church functioned and grew in the first decades.

Christ had instructed the apostles to go out and teach others what he had taught them, and they did just that. Through their teaching, the number of Christians grew prodigiously from the beginning. Christ had also instructed his followers to baptise new converts, as the ceremony by which they would become members of the Church, and throughout the Acts we see this happening. Since then, baptism has been administered to all people entering the Church.

Moreover, on the night before he died, Christ instituted what is called the Eucharist, the sacrifice of the worship of God, during which he changed bread and wine into his body and blood and he instructed the apostles to continue to do this. Paul describes it in his first letter to the Church in Corinth: "For I received from the Lord what I also delivered to you, that the Lord Jesus on the night when he was betrayed took bread, and when he had given thanks, he broke it, and said, 'This is my body which is for you. Do this in remembrance of me.' In the same way also the chalice, after supper, saying, 'This chalice is the new covenant in my blood. Do this, as often as you drink it, in remembrance of me.' For as often as you eat this bread and drink the chalice, you proclaim the Lord's death until he comes. Whoever, therefore, eats the bread or drinks the cup of the Lord in an unworthy manner will be guilty of profaning the body and blood of the Lord" (*1 Cor* 11:23-27).

From then on, the apostles began to celebrate the Eucharist, known in the early Church as the "breaking of the bread" (cf. *Acts* 2:46, 20:7), and more commonly known now as the Mass. It was the new way of worshiping God, and it replaced the daily sacrifices of animals which the Jews had carried out since the time of Moses, some 1200 years before.

When Christ said that the bread was now his body, and the wine was now his blood, he meant just that. The early Church believed, and the Catholic Church has continued to believe and teach, that the host received in Communion during Mass is truly the body and blood of Christ. As evidence of this, over the centuries there have been numerous Eucharistic miracles, where the wafer, or host, which was formerly bread, was changed into blood and human tissue. One of the first of these miracles took place in the Italian city of Lanciano in the eighth century.

More recently there have been Eucharistic miracles in Buenos Aires, Argentina, in 1996, Tixtla, Mexico in 2006, and the Polish cities of Sokołka in 2008 and Legnica in 2013. In each of these cases, the host turned into a substance which, when examined under a microscope by scientists, was identified as human tissue from the heart. Moreover, some of the scientists determined that the person from whom the tissue was taken had suffered trauma similar to that which a person goes through in the final agony before death. This is consistent with the belief that the host was the body of Christ as he hung on the cross in the crucifixion. Added to that is the extraordinary phenomenon of the blood on the host being type AB, the same type as in the miracle of Lanciano and on the Shroud of Turin. That type is very rare – less than one per cent of the general population has it – but it is quite common in the Middle East. All of these miracles took place in Catholic churches.

Another rite that Christ gave his Church is that of the forgiveness of sins by a priest. He did it on the evening of his resurrection, when he appeared to the apostles. St John relates in his gospel: "On the evening of that day, the first day of the week, the doors being shut where the disciples were, for fear of the Jews, Jesus came and stood among them and said to them, 'Peace be with you.'… And when he had said this, he breathed on them, and said to them, 'Receive the Holy Spirit. If you forgive the sins of any, they are forgiven; if you retain the sins of any, they are retained'" (*John* 20:19-23).

The Catholic Church has continued to celebrate this rite ever since. The priest forgives sins in the name of God, who is the only one who can forgive them. It is a great source of peace and joy to know that one's sins have been forgiven, that the burden of sin has been lifted.

Another important feature of the Church founded by Christ is the fact that it was to have one person as its head, with authority over the whole Church. That person, named by Christ himself, was Peter. The acceptance of Peter's authority by the other apostles is seen clearly in such facts as that he is always mentioned first when the gospels give the names of the apostles. And in the Acts of the Apostles it is Peter who proposes the election of someone to replace the apostle Judas (cf. *Acts* 1:15-26), who speaks at length to the multitudes gathered in Jerusalem for the feast of Pentecost (cf. *Acts* 2:14-42), and who draws the other apostles with him in deciding in the Council of Jerusalem what to impose on gentile converts to the Church (cf. *Acts* 15:1-21).

When Peter was put to death under the emperor Nero in Rome around the year 65 AD, a man named Linus was chosen to succeed him. Linus was followed by Cletus and then Clement, and so on down to our own day. The head of the Catholic Church is called the Pope, and he can trace his origin back in an unbroken line to the apostle Peter, who was appointed by Christ himself. By the time of the election of Pope Francis in 2013, there had been 266 Popes.

Although Christ's Church was a single body for the first centuries, with the passing of the years different parts of it broke away to form separate communities. The most important were the Coptic Orthodox and a few other communities following the Council of Chalcedon in 451, the Eastern Orthodox Churches (Greek, Russian, Romanian, etc.) in 1054, and the Anglican and numerous Protestant denominations in the sixteenth century. Various issues brought this about, which we needn't go into here.

All of these denominations are indeed Christian, and they have retained to varying degrees the teachings and practices which Christ gave his Church. The Orthodox especially are very close to the Catholic Church in this regard, although they do not accept the authority of the Pope.

Altogether, Christians make up almost one third of the world's population, with some 2.4 billion adherents. More than half of these are Catholic, some 1.3 billion.

Over the centuries the Catholic Church has continued to delve ever deeper into the truths taught by Jesus Christ and to interpret and explain them to others. From the beginning this was done by great saints like St Augustine and St Thomas Aquinas, by Popes, by gatherings of bishops from all over the world in what are known as Ecumenical Councils, etc. This work goes on today. As the fruit of it, the Church has developed a rich body of teaching, including on the question of life after death. An important official document containing the most important teachings of the Church is the *Catechism of the Catholic Church,* which was first published in 1992. We will use that document, and others, to study the Church's teaching on the question of life after death.

As I have said, you may not believe everything that the Catholic Church teaches. That is up to you. But this teaching does come from an authoritative source – Jesus Christ, who showed by his words and deeds that he was indeed God – and from the Church he founded. It makes sense at least to hear what this Church has to say about life after death. We will begin with the question of death itself.

12

Death

They say that the only certainties in life are death and taxes. Some people have found ingenious ways to avoid paying taxes, but no one can avoid death. It is certain, for all of us. At some time in the future, we usually have no idea when or how, we will die. The funeral will be ours.

For many people, the very thought of death, not to mention its reality, is something frightening, forbidding, something they don't even want to think about. Blaise Pascal expresses it well: "Instability. It is a horrible thing to feel all that we possess slipping away" (*Pensées*, n. 212). Perhaps it is the uncertainty of how death will come about and of what happens after it, or the pain and discomfort that sometimes accompanies it, the loss of control, or the thought of leaving loved ones behind... All of that can be very true and somewhat discomfiting. But in reality, the more we come to know about death and what awaits us on the other side, the less we fear it. We may even look forward to it.

We can start from the experience of the many people who have had near-death experiences, in which they found themselves in a state of indescribable joy, peace and love, where they would have preferred to stay rather than return to earth. Many of them said, after the experience, that they no longer feared death. They realised it is just a threshold we have to pass through on the way to eternal life with God.

That is the way the Catholic Church looks on it too. Taking up the common, and understandable, trepidation of many people at the thought of death, the bishops of the Church, gathered in the Second Vatican Council in Rome from 1962 to 1965, stated:

> It is in the face of death that the riddle of human existence grows most acute. Not only is man tormented by pain and by the advancing deterioration of his body, but even more so by a dread of perpetual extinction. He rightly follows the intuition of his heart when he abhors and repudiates the utter ruin and total disappearance of his own person. He rebels against death because he bears in himself an eternal seed which cannot be reduced to sheer matter. All the endeavours of technology, though useful in the extreme, cannot calm his anxiety; for prolongation of biological life is unable to satisfy that desire for higher life which is inescapably lodged in his breast (*Gaudium et Spes,* n. 18).

As the bishops go on to say, while the person naturally abhors the deterioration of his body and the disappearance of his person, yet there is something in him, an "eternal seed", which is not mere matter and which cries out for a higher life:

> Although the mystery of death utterly beggars the imagination, the Church has been taught by divine revelation and firmly teaches that man has been created by God for a blissful purpose beyond the reach of earthly misery. In addition, that bodily death, from which man would have been immune had he not sinned, will be vanquished, according to the Christian faith, when man, who was ruined by his own doing, is restored to wholeness by an almighty and merciful Saviour. For God has called man and still calls him so that, with his entire being, he might be joined to him in an endless sharing of a divine life beyond all corruption. Christ won this victory when he rose to life, for by his death he freed man from death. Hence, to every thoughtful man, a

solidly established faith provides the answer to his anxiety about what the future holds for him. At the same time faith gives him the power to be united in Christ with his loved ones who have already been snatched away by death; faith arouses the hope that they have found true life with God (*ibid.*).

As this text says, death has a positive meaning in that even Jesus Christ, the Son of God, died so that he might free mankind from death, in the sense of freeing us from eternal separation from God. By his death on the cross of Calvary and by his resurrection from the dead, Christ opened the way for us to be with him forever in heaven, "joined to him in an endless sharing of a divine life beyond all corruption". The *Catechism of the Catholic Church* expresses it succinctly: "For those who die in Christ's grace, it is a participation in the death of the Lord, so that they can also share his Resurrection" (*CCC* 1006).

For those unfamiliar with this topic, it is the understanding that the first human beings, called Adam and Eve in the Bible, offended God by what is called the original sin, and that, as a result, their offspring down the ages were unable to go to heaven when they died. They became subject to suffering and death, and they had a certain disordered tendency to sin. We are all aware of our sinfulness. But God sent his Son Jesus to redeem all mankind and restore them to friendship with God, opening up the way to eternal life with him. Christ accomplished this by his death on the cross and by his resurrection from the dead.

The Catechism goes on to say: "Death is transformed by Christ. Jesus, the Son of God, also himself suffered the death that is part of the human condition. Yet, despite his anguish as he faced death, he accepted it in an act of complete and free submission to his Father's will. The obedience of Jesus has transformed the curse of death into a blessing" (*CCC* 1009). Yes death, for those who live and die well, is truly a blessing, for it is the passage into blissful union with God for all eternity.

In answer to those who believe that we can die more than once, returning to life reincarnated in a different form, the Christian view is clear. We die only once. The Letter to the Hebrews says that "it is appointed for men to die once, and after that comes judgment" (*Heb* 9:27). The Catechism explains: "Death is the end of man's earthly pilgrimage, of the time of grace and mercy which God offers him so as to work out his earthly life in keeping with the divine plan, and to decide his ultimate destiny. When 'the single course of our earthly life' is completed, we shall not return to other earthly lives: 'It is appointed for men to die once.' There is no 'reincarnation' after death" (*CCC* 1013).

In view of this, since we have only one life to live here on earth, we must use it wisely. Depending on how we live, and how we die, we decide our ultimate destiny, whether the bliss and love of eternal life with God in heaven, or eternal separation from God and punishment in hell. The near-death experiences of many reveal that it was their own free choices that destined them to hell or heaven. We should endeavour always to make the right choices. Pope Benedict XVI reminds us how important this is: "With death, our life-choice becomes definitive" (Enc. *Spe Salvi,* n. 45). Once we die, we cannot go back and change our mind, let alone our life. It is too late to repent of our bad choices. We must do it while we are alive. The Catechism makes clear that "there is no repentance for men after death" (*CCC* 393).

And since we don't know how long we have to live – we could die tomorrow from a heart attack or an accident – we cannot put off making whatever changes may be necessary to prepare ourselves. In this sense the words of Thomas à Kempis, in his fifteenth-century classic *The Imitation of Christ*, are especially helpful:

> Every action of yours, every thought, should be those of one

who expects to die before the day is out. Death would have no great terrors for you if you had a quiet conscience... Then why not keep clear of sin instead of running away from death? If you aren't fit to face death today, it's very unlikely you will be tomorrow (*Imitation...*, 1, 23, 1).

For our own age, when many people go to great lengths to live longer and delay dying, St Augustine (354-430) has some wise words: "If men go to so much trouble and effort to live here a little longer, ought they not strive so much harder to live eternally?" (*De verb. Dom. Serm.*, 64)

While we tend to speak of death as if it were the end of life, it is not the end but the beginning of life in a different form. Our short life on earth comes to an end, yes, but our life goes on, in eternity. And we do not fall asleep, never to wake up, but rather we remain conscious, aware of what is happening. We see this in near-death experiences, where a person's soul leaves the body and hovers above it, fully aware of what is going on in the efforts of resuscitation, and sometimes trying to communicate with those involved, but unable to do so. It is also seen in those who experience their life review, or judgment, completely aware of what they are seeing, and in those who go to heaven and encounter loved ones. The soul lives on. It is awake and conscious, not asleep.

St Cyprian, a bishop who died a martyr in North Africa in 258, expresses beautifully the passage from life on earth to life hereafter: "What an honour, what happiness to depart joyfully from this world, to go forth in glory from the anguish and pain, in one moment to close the eyes that looked on the world of men and in the next to open them at once to look on God and Christ! The speed of this joyous departure! You are suddenly withdrawn from earth to find yourself in the kingdom of heaven" (*Tract. Ad Fortunatum*, ch. 13).

Thoughts like these can lead a good-living person to look forward to dying, whenever that may come, rather than to fear it. An outstanding example is the second-century martyr St Ignatius of Antioch. On his way to Rome in chains, sentenced to be torn apart by wild animals, he wrote: "Here and now, as I write in the fulness of life, I am yearning for death with all the passion of a lover. Earthly longings have been crucified; in me there is left no spark of desire for mundane things, but only a murmur of living water that whispers within me, 'Come to the Father'" (*Letter to the Romans*, 6, 1-9, 3).

In the sixteenth century, St Teresa of Avila (1515-1582) expressed the same thought: "I want to see God and, in order to see him, I must die" (*Life,* Ch. 1). And St Thérèse of Lisieux (1873-1897) said: "I am not dying; I am entering life" (*The Last Conversations)*.

Indeed, when we look on it this way, death is not something to be feared. It is rather to be desired, being merely the passage of the soul to a new state of existence. If we live well, we will die well and we too can look forward to God's call to join him in heaven for all eternity.

But first, immediately after we die we will face God in the life review, which Christians call the particular judgment.

13

The Life Review

As we have seen, many people in their near-death experiences have gone through what has come to be called the life review, where they see their whole life in an instant. All is laid bare before them: their good deeds and their bad ones. Some people were even allowed to experience what other people felt when they insulted or hurt them, or helped them, in some way. And they realise that what they are seeing is the truth. There is no room for the excuses they may have had when they did the wrong thing in life. Here they must accept the reality of their life as they lived it.

This life review is what is known in Christian terminology as the particular judgment. It is the judgment of each soul immediately after death, in the presence of God. As the Letter to the Hebrews says, "it is appointed for men to die once, and after that comes judgment" (*Heb* 9:27). And St Paul, in his second letter to the Corinthians, says: "For we must all appear before the judgment seat of Christ, so that each one may receive good or evil, according to what he has done in the body" (*2 Cor* 5:10).

St Paul may very well be describing the judgment when he writes to the Christians in Corinth, comparing being judged by others with being judged by God:

> But with me it is a very small thing that I should be judged
> by you or by any human court. I do not even judge myself. I

am not aware of anything against myself, but I am not thereby acquitted. It is the Lord who judges me. Therefore, do not pronounce judgment before the time, before the Lord comes, who will bring to light the things now hidden in darkness and will disclose the purposes of the heart. Then every man will receive his commendation from God (*1 Cor* 4:3-5).

Paul says that he cannot even judge himself. When he scrutinises his conduct, he does not find anything against himself, but that does not justify him before God. It is God who will judge him. And it is God who will judge us. He will bring to light things hidden in darkness, deeds we have forgotten about completely, both good and bad. And he will reveal the purposes, the motives, that moved us to do what we did.

All of this is telling us that the life review, the particular judgment, will be thorough, complete, objective. We will not be able to hide anything. All will be brought to light. Nor will we be able to come with excuses, as if to justify our conduct. We will accept what we see, because we will acknowledge that, before God, it is the truth.

Paul concludes the passage saying that after the judgment every man will receive his commendation from God. That is, on the basis of what is revealed to us in the judgment, our soul will pass immediately to its reward or punishment, which we will consider in the following chapters. At the moment of death our time for determining our eternal destiny comes to an end. It is too late to change anything. Even those who have had a near-death experience of hell say that they realised in the judgment that that was what they deserved. It was their choices in life that made them deserve that destiny.

Again, we see how important it is to live well, so that we can die well and deserve eternal life with God. If we have made bad choices, there is still time, as long as we are alive, to repent and change our ways. The *Catechism of the Catholic Church* teaches: "Death puts an end to human life as the time open to either accepting or rejecting the divine grace manifested in Christ. The New Testament … repeatedly affirms that each will be rewarded immediately after death in accordance with his works and faith" (*CCC* 1021).

St Jerome, who died in 420 AD and translated the Bible into Latin, expresses this same idea. He says that "what will happen to all on the day of judgment, has already taken place for each one on the day of their death" (*In Joel,* 2:1). With death, our eternal destiny has already been decided.

As regards the reward or punishment that awaits us, the Catechism continues: "Each man receives his eternal retribution in his immortal soul at the very moment of his death, in a particular judgment that refers his life to Christ: either entrance into the blessedness of heaven – through a purification, or immediately – or immediate and everlasting damnation" (*CCC* 1022).

In another passage from the New Testament, Jesus Christ tells us that he himself will be our judge:

> Truly, truly, I say to you, the hour is coming, and now is, when the dead will hear the voice of the Son of God, and those who hear will live. For as the Father has life in himself, so he has granted the Son also to have life in himself, and has given him authority to execute judgment, because he is the Son of man. Do not marvel at this; for the hour is coming when all who are in the tombs will hear his voice, and come forth, those who have done good, to the resurrection of life, and those who have done evil, to the resurrection of judgment. I can do nothing on my own authority; as I hear, I judge; and my judgment is just, because I seek not my own will but the will of him who sent me (*John* 5:25-30).

As Christ says, he, the Son of man, will be our judge. He often called himself the Son of man, a title that goes back to the Old Testament. As he was born of Mary, he is truly man, truly human, and so he knows our human nature, with all its weaknesses. It is thus consoling to know that we will be judged by one who is human like us, as well as being, of course, God.

A particular, and exceedingly helpful, experience of the judgment is related by Raymond Moody, in his book *The Light Beyond*. It concerns a man who was living a criminal life when he was struck by lightning one day on the golf course and "died". He had a near-death experience in which he passed through a tunnel into a bright pastoral setting where he met a being of light that he called "God", who led him through a life review. In it, he relived his entire life, not only seeing his actions but feeling their effects on others. The experience changed him completely, for the better. He felt that when he really died he would have to undergo the life review again and it would be very uncomfortable if he didn't learn from the first one (pp. 33-34).

Following our life review, or particular judgment, our soul will pass immediately to its eternal reward or punishment. As suggested in the near-death experiences of so many, this will be either eternal happiness in heaven, or eternal punishment in hell. If the person is destined for heaven but the soul is not yet sufficiently purified, it will undergo this purification in the state we call purgatory.

So now let us look at the three possible states of the soul immediately after death: heaven, purgatory and hell.

14

Heaven

The goal of life, the reason why we are here on earth, is to prepare for the next life, for eternal life – in heaven. As we have seen throughout this book, we have a spiritual soul, and it longs for, is made for, something beyond what it can attain in this life. That longing is satisfied only in heaven, and there it is truly satisfied. Here on earth we long for happiness and we find it up to a point. But our happiness here comes and goes, and it varies in intensity. Some things give us more happiness than others. We were made for something more, for complete happiness. And we will have it in heaven.

The numerous near-death experiences, where people found themselves in a state of absolute bliss, peace and love point to this. Those who have had this experience often say that when they came back to life on earth they realised that life here is not the end, but just the preparation for the next life. And they said they would have preferred to stay in that blissful state, even more than to come back to be with their family or to take care of their unfinished business on earth. They had this experience not as some sort of fantasy, or a dream of an unreal and unrealisable world, but rather as something real, a foretaste of what awaits us if we live and die well. The fact that so many people, of different ages and religious beliefs, have had the same experience points to a reality, not a fantasy.

Yes, heaven is for real. We have not only human experience to suggest that it is real, but also the very word of God in Scripture. Jesus Christ himself promises it to those who live charity on earth. In his description of the judgment, he speaks of the Son of man coming to judge mankind and saying to those on his right hand: "Come, O blessed of my Father, inherit the kingdom prepared for you from the foundation of the world; for I was hungry and you gave me food, I was thirsty and you gave me drink, I was a stranger and you welcomed me ... And they will go away ... into eternal life" (*Matthew* 25:34-46).

Christ also speaks of heaven to his apostles on the night before he died on the cross. In what we call the Last Supper, he told them: "In my Father's house are many rooms; if it were not so, would I have told you that I go to prepare a place for you? And when I go and prepare a place for you, I will come again and will take you to myself, that where I am you may be also" (*John* 14:2-3). This is a beautiful image of heaven: a room in the Father's house. When we die, we go home, to the house of our heavenly Father. A few hours before he died on 2 April 2005, Pope John Paul II said to those with him, "Let me go to the Father's house."

The joy of heaven is indescribable. St Paul, who felt himself caught up one day into heaven, could not describe the joy and beauty of what he experienced there. He could only say that he "heard things that cannot be told, which man may not utter: (*2 Cor* 12:2-4). On another occasion he wrote of it: "What no eye has seen, nor ear heard, nor the heart of man conceived, what God has prepared for those who love him" (*1 Cor* 9:9).

St Paul also describes heaven as seeing God face to face: "For now we see in a mirror dimly, but then face to face. Now I know in part; then I shall understand fully, even as I have been fully understood" (*1 Cor* 13:12). As he says, here on earth we know God only in part, through the world he has made, and through what he has revealed to us in Jesus Christ and the Scriptures. We can only imagine what it would be like to behold God's majesty, his infinite beauty, and to do so directly, face to face. In heaven we will do that.

If we wonder how we will be able to see God face to face when he is pure spirit, we can begin by remembering that when people in near-death experiences saw heaven, they sometimes recognised their loved ones there, even though those loved ones were there not in their body but only in their soul. It will be the same with seeing God. The understanding is that we will be given a special help, known as the Light of Glory, to see him. In any case, what is certain is that the most important aspect of our joy in heaven will be being with God in all his glory and knowing ourselves loved by him, with unimaginable love.

The last book of the Bible, the book of Revelation, echoes this idea, saying that the souls in heaven: "shall see his face, and his name shall be on their foreheads. And night shall be no more; they need no light of lamp or sun, for the Lord God will be their light, and they shall reign for ever and ever" (*Rev* 22:4-5). That same book also describes the vast number and immense joy of those in heaven:

> After this I looked, and behold, a great multitude which no man could number, from every nation, from all tribes and peoples and tongues, standing before the throne and before the Lamb, clothed in white robes, with palm branches in their hands, and crying out with a loud voice, 'Salvation belongs to our God who sits upon the throne, and to the Lamb... They shall hunger no more, neither thirst any more; the sun shall not strike them, nor any scorching heat. For the Lamb in the midst of the throne will be their shepherd, and he will guide them to springs of living water; and God will wipe away every tear from their eyes (*Rev* 7:9-10, 16-17).

The Lamb of course, is Jesus Christ himself, who was called the Lamb of God. Compared with the joy that awaits us in heaven, any suffering we can undergo on earth is as nothing. St Paul, who experienced frequent and intense suffering on earth – scourging, being beaten with rods, being stoned, shipwreck, cold, heat, hunger, thirst – says: "I consider that the sufferings of this present time are not worth comparing with the glory that is to be revealed to us" (*Rom* 8:18).

The teaching of the Church, developed over the centuries, is expressed in the *Catechism of the Catholic Church:* "Those who die in God's grace and friendship and are perfectly purified live for ever with Christ. They are like God for ever, for they 'see him as he is,' face to face" (*CCC* 1023).

The Catechism goes on to summarise all this, describing the joy of heaven: "This perfect life with the Most Holy Trinity – this communion of life and love with the Trinity, with the Virgin Mary, the angels and all the blessed – is called 'heaven'. Heaven is the ultimate end and fulfilment of the deepest human longings, the state of supreme, definitive happiness" (*CCC* 1024).

As this point says, the greatest source of joy in heaven will be sharing in the communion of life and love with God himself, who reveals himself as a trinity of persons: Father, Son and Holy Spirit, in one God. In addition, those in heaven will delight in the presence of Jesus' mother Mary, the angels, and the vast number of the blessed, all those who, over the centuries, have died and gone to heaven. Among them will be members of our own families and friends who have preceded us in death. It will be like an immense family reunion.

What is more, heaven is "the ultimate end and fulfilment of the deepest human longings". As we saw earlier, our human longings are never fully satisfied here on earth. We long for more than we can possibly attain here below. There is something in us, our spiritual soul, which is in some way unlimited, which cannot be satisfied with the limited goods we can find on earth. Only in heaven will we find the complete happiness we long for. Not for nothing did St Augustine write to God: "You made us for you, and our heart is restless until it rests in you" (*Confessions,* 1, 1, 1). Only in God, who is the infinite good, will our heart truly rest.

And heaven is the state of "supreme, definitive happiness". It is supreme, the highest possible. On earth we have much happiness, very much, but it is not the total happiness we seek. There is a reason for this. We find happiness when we find a good. The good might be a loving spouse, a good meal, a good book, a good holiday, a new house, a new car... All of these are finite, limited goods which cannot satisfy the unlimited longing of our heart. As evidence of this, some of the richest people, who seem to have everything, are very unhappy. Only the infinite good, God himself, can truly satisfy us.

Our happiness in heaven is not only supreme, it is "definitive", everlasting, without ever lessening. Again, on earth our happiness comes and goes: the good film ends, we finish the book or the holiday, our new car wears out... But not in heaven. We will be in union with God and all the blessed forever. Our happiness will not end, nor will it lessen in any way. This is difficult to imagine, but we have God's word that this is how it will be. It is truly something to look forward to.

The Catechism goes on to express the beauty and joy of heaven: "This mystery of blessed communion with God and all who are in Christ is beyond all understanding and description. Scripture speaks of it in images: life, light, peace, wedding feast, wine of the kingdom, the Father's house, the heavenly Jerusalem, paradise: 'no eye has seen, nor ear heard, nor the heart of man conceived, what God has prepared for those who love him'" (*1 Cor* 2:9; *CCC* 1027).

The idea of eternal life in heaven may suggest to us that it may somehow be boring, always the same. This might be the case if eternity were an endless succession of time. But it is not. Pope Benedict XVI writes of it in his encyclical *Spe salvi*:

> It would be like plunging into the ocean of infinite love, a moment in which time—the before and after—no longer exists. We can only attempt to grasp the idea that such a moment is life in the full sense, a plunging ever anew into the vastness of being, in which we are simply overwhelmed with joy. This is how Jesus expresses it in Saint John's gospel: "I will see you again and your hearts will rejoice, and no one will take your joy from you" (*John* 16:22; *SS* n. 12).

In view of the overwhelming joy that is heaven, it is worthwhile to sacrifice everything that takes us away from God, and to endeavour to live a good life, so that one day we will be with God forever.

Who can go to heaven? Must one be a Christian, or a believer in some other religion, or at least a believer in God? The short answer is that, in principle, everyone can go to heaven. St Paul writes that God "desires all men to be saved and to come to the knowledge of the truth" (*1 Tim* 2:4). God created every human being in his image and likeness and his plan is that everyone should be with him in paradise. He excludes no one. Some may exclude themselves, as we will see when we study hell, but that is their own choosing, not God's.

The Catholic Church, in the Second Vatican Council, addressed this question. After considering the relationship of the Church to many different groups of people – other Christians, Jews, Muslims, those who do not know Christ – it finished with those who do not even know God, declaring: "Nor shall divine providence deny the assistance necessary for salvation to those who, without any fault of theirs, have not yet arrived at an explicit knowledge of God, and who, not without grace, strive to lead a good life. Whatever good or truth is found amongst them is considered by the Church to be a preparation for the gospel and given by him who enlightens all men that they may at length have life" (*LG* 16).

As this point says, even those who do not know God can be saved and go to heaven. They must be in this position through no fault of their own and they must strive to lead a good life, which includes being sorry for their wrongdoing, or sins. What is more, God will give them, and everyone, all the grace, the help they need to go to heaven. Now it is up to them – to each one of us. Our eternal destiny is in our hands.

15

Purgatory

If someone dies with sorrow for their sins they will be saved, but they may first have to undergo purification before they are ready for heaven. This purification of the soul is undergone in a state that has come to be called purgatory. We have already mentioned it in the near-death experience of Gloria Polo and in the reference to the numerous souls in purgatory who have appeared to people on earth over the centuries. But, you might ask, wherever did we get the idea of purgatory?

Allusions to purgatory in the Bible

Belief in the purification of the soul after death goes back to the beginning of the Church. Really, it goes back to the Old Testament, to the Second Book of the Maccabees, written in the second century BC. There we read how the Maccabean leader Judas, discovering that his soldiers who had been killed in battle were all wearing tokens of false gods, prayed that their sins might be forgiven. He then took up a collection to be sent to Jerusalem to have a sacrifice offered for them. "In doing this he acted very well and honourably, taking account of the resurrection. For if he were not expecting that those who had fallen would rise again, it would have been superfluous and foolish to pray for the dead. But if he was looking to the splendid reward that is laid up for those who fall asleep in godliness, it was a holy and pious thought. Therefore he made atonement for the dead, that they might be delivered from their sin" (*2 Mac* 12:43-45). This passage clearly attests to the belief of the Jews at that time that there was a resurrection of the dead, and that those who had died could be helped to be freed from their sins after death by sacrifices and prayers offered for them. In other words, that there is a state of purification of the soul after death. This is what we now call purgatory.

While the New Testament is not explicit in teaching about purgatory, various texts allude to it. The book of Revelation, for example, says that "nothing unclean shall enter" the heavenly Jerusalem (*Rev* 21:27). A similar text is found in the Letter to the Hebrews, which reads: "Strive for peace with all men, and for the holiness without which no one will see the Lord" (*Heb* 12:14). Both of these texts are telling us that in order to enter heaven, where all is light, purity, holiness, love, the soul must be perfectly pure, without any stain of sin. This is understandable in human terms. If we were invited to a dinner or reception with an important person, we would put on our best clothes and make sure they were spotlessly clean. How much more important it is, then, for the soul to be without any stain of sin in order to enter into the presence of the all-holy God in heaven.

Jesus himself says in the Sermon on the Mount, with regard to someone in debt to another: "Make friends quickly with your accuser, while you are going with him to court, lest your accuser hand you over to the judge, and the judge to the guard, and you be put in prison; truly, I say to you, you will never get out till you have paid the last penny" (*Matthew* 5:25-26). While in itself this text cannot prove anything regarding purgatory, it has been used to speak about a debt before God owing for sin, which must be paid in full before the soul is free to go to heaven. In the second century the writer Tertullian, for example, understands by prison the realm of the dead, and by the last penny, the sins that must be atoned for before the person can go to heaven (cf. *De anima* 58).

Still another New Testament text that alludes to purgatory is from St Paul, who writes that each person builds his life on the foundation of Jesus Christ and, in the judgment, the quality of his work will be "revealed with fire, and the fire will test what sort of work each one has done. If the work which any man has built on the foundation survives, he will receive a reward. If any man's work is burned up, he will suffer loss, though he himself will be saved, but only as through fire" (*1 Cor* 3:13-15). The Western Fathers of the Church understood this passage as referring to a purifying punishment by fire in the next life, and hence to purgatory (cf. St Augustine, *Enarr. in Ps.* 37, 3; St Caesarius of Arles, *Sermo* 179).

Belief in purgatory in the early Church

Independently of what we find in Scripture, the tradition in the early Church of praying for those who have died so that they may be purified of their sins is overwhelming. Writings on tombstones and in the catacombs include such inscriptions as: "May you have eternal life in Christ", "May he rest in peace," "Eternal light shine upon thee, Timothea, in Christ", and "Thee, O heavenly Father, we implore to have mercy." If the early Christians thought everyone who had died went straight to heaven, they would not have prayed for them.

Around the year 216 Tertullian describes how the Church prayed for the dead and offered Mass for them on the anniversary of their death: "A woman, after the death of her husband ... prays for his soul and asks that he may, while waiting, find rest; and that he may share in the first resurrection. And each year, on the anniversary of his death, she offers the sacrifice" (*Monogamy* 10:1–2). The sacrifice is, of course, the celebration of the Mass.

In the middle of the fourth century, St Cyril of Jerusalem writes of prayers for the dead in the Mass: "Then we make mention ... of all among us who have already fallen asleep, for we believe that it will be of very great benefit to the souls of those for whom the petition is carried up, while this holy and most solemn sacrifice is laid out" (*Catechetical Lectures* 23:5:9).

Around the year 392 St John Chrysostom writes of the souls of the deceased: "Let us help and commemorate them. If Job's sons were purified by their father's sacrifice (cf. *Job* 1:5), why would we doubt that our offerings for the dead bring them some consolation? Let us not hesitate to help those who have died and to offer our prayers for them" (*Homilies on First Corinthians* 41:5).

Well known is St Monica's request to her son St Augustine just before her death: "Lay this body anywhere...This only I ask of you, that you remember me at the altar of the Lord, wherever you may be" (St Augustine, *Confessions* 9, 10-11).

St Augustine himself, around the year 421, wrote: "That there should be some fire even after this life is not incredible, and it can be inquired into and either be discovered or left hidden whether some of the faithful may be saved, some more slowly and some more quickly in the greater or lesser degree in which they loved the good things that perish, through a certain purgatorial fire" (*Handbook on Faith, Hope, and Charity* 18:69).

St Caesarius of Arles, who died in 452, said in a sermon: "If we neither give thanks to God in tribulations nor redeem our own sins by good works, we shall have to remain in that purgatorial fire as long as it takes the aforesaid lesser sins to be consumed" (*Sermon* 179, 2).

In short, so widespread was the custom of praying and offering

Masses for the dead, that St Isidore of Seville could write in the seventh century: "To offer the sacrifice for the repose of the faithful departed is a custom observed all over the world. For this reason we believe that it is a custom taught by the very apostles" (*On ecclesiastical offices,* 1).

These texts are just a handful of the many that could be cited from the early Church. It is clear from them that the custom of praying and offering Masses for the dead, based on the belief in a state of purification of the soul after death, was universally accepted and practised in the early centuries. Even if there were nothing at all in the Bible about it, we would still believe in it as coming from the life and practice of the Church.

The teaching of the Church

Purgatory is a reality, not just a pious belief. What does the Church say about it? In the *Catechism of the Catholic Church* we read: "All who die in God's grace and friendship, but still imperfectly purified, are indeed assured of their eternal salvation; but after death they undergo purification, so as to achieve the holiness necessary to enter the joy of heaven" (*CCC* 1030). Again, we see here how the soul must be completely purified, holy, in order to enter heaven. The person has died "in God's grace and friendship", that is, with sorrow for their sins and love for God, so that they are assured of going to heaven, but their soul is not yet perfectly purified from the effects of sin. This purification takes place in the state we call purgatory.

The understanding is that, in addition to asking God to forgive our sins, we must do something to make up for the harm caused to God and the Church by our sins. That is, sin leaves a certain debt to be paid to God's justice and holiness before the soul is perfectly purified and ready for heaven. In his mercy, God does not ask that we make up wholly for the harm our sins have caused to his infinite majesty and love, for we could never do that. But we must do something. This is understandable. If we damage the property of another and ask to be forgiven, the owner may forgive us, but he will still want us to pay for the damage we have caused. Apart from the need to make up in some way for this debt to God caused by our sins, we also need to make up for any lack of sorrow for lesser sins, and for the bad habits and attachments caused by our sins.

We can do this here on earth by all our good works, prayers, acts of self-denial, etc. And, of course, the Church grants the remission of some or all of this debt when we do certain prescribed acts through what are called indulgences. If when we die we haven't made up completely for our sins, we must do it in purgatory. It is for this reason too, that the Church has had from the early centuries the season of Lent, leading up to Easter, when all are invited to do special acts of penance, or self-denial, to make up for their sins.

St Catherine of Genoa (1447-1510), describes purgatory like this: "No one is barred from heaven. Whoever wants to enter heaven may do so because God is all-merciful. Our Lord will welcome us into glory with his arms wide open. The Almighty is so pure, however, that if a person is conscious of the least trace of imperfection and at the same time understands that purgatory is ordained to do away with such impediments, the soul enters this place of purification glad to accept so great a mercy of God. The worst suffering of these suffering souls is to have sinned against divine Goodness and not to have been purified in this life" (*Treatise on Purgatory,* 12).

The two principal pains of purgatory are the pain of loss, of being deprived of the sight of God, and the pain of sense, likened to fire. All agree that the greatest of these pains is that of loss. This makes sense. When someone loves another intensely and cannot be with their beloved, they suffer greatly. In purgatory, as the soul's disordered love for the world and for itself is gradually purged, the love for God grows proportionately, and at the end it is so great that the suffering of not being with God is very intense.

The souls in purgatory welcome their suffering because it purifies them for their entry into heaven, of which they are assured. Not for nothing does the Church call them the "blessed souls" in Purgatory. Pope Benedict XVI speaks of this suffering as arising from the encounter of the soul with the love of Christ. In his encyclical *Spe salvi*, on hope, he writes: "This encounter with [Christ], as it burns us, transforms and frees us, allowing us to become truly ourselves... His gaze, the touch of his heart heals us through an undeniably painful transformation 'as through fire'. But it is a blessed pain, in which the holy power of his love sears through us like a flame, enabling us to become totally ourselves and thus totally of God... The pain of love becomes our salvation and our joy" (*SS*, 47).

At the same time, the souls in purgatory are exceedingly happy, for they are assured of heaven. Indeed, purgatory is the happiest place outside of heaven. The souls there rejoice even in their suffering, knowing that it speeds up their entry into heaven. It is like a person who has just emerged from surgery, wracked with pain but with the joy of knowing they will now recover their health. Confirmation of the great joy experienced by the souls in purgatory comes from an elderly nun, who while in purgatory appeared to a monk and said: "The greatest happiness for a soul is to be in heaven. It is eternal bliss. But immediately after this, there is no joy greater than to savour the joys of purgatory" (*Visions of Purgatory,* Scepter 2014, p. 154). This nun was in purgatory herself. She would know.

The Catechism continues: "From the beginning the Church has honoured the memory of the dead and offered prayers in suffrage for them, above all the Eucharistic sacrifice, so that, thus purified, they may attain the beatific vision of God. The Church also commends almsgiving, indulgences and works of penance undertaken on behalf of the dead" (*CCC* 1032).

While the souls in purgatory can do nothing to shorten their own suffering, we on earth can help to lessen it by the prayers and sacrifices we offer for them. This is the reason for the many prayers, penances and Masses which have been offered for the souls in purgatory since the beginning of the Church. Souls in purgatory have often said that the greatest help they receive is from the Mass, which is the sacrifice of Christ's death on the cross made present on the altar.

Although the souls in purgatory cannot help themselves, they can pray for those they leave behind here on earth. This is only natural. A mother or father who dies will continue to pray for their family members just as they did when they were on earth. And their prayer is more powerful in purgatory than it was on earth, since there they are now closer to God.

For this reason, it is appropriate too to ask the souls in purgatory to intercede before God for our intentions. They are powerful intercessors. St Catherine of Bologna (1413-1463), who was very devoted to the souls in purgatory, was certain that her prayers to the holy souls were answered. She writes: "I received many and very great favours from the saints, but still greater favours from the holy souls."

The duration and intensity of the suffering in purgatory differs for each soul. For some it may be only a few minutes or days; for others, years. This is borne out by the numerous apparitions of souls in purgatory to people on earth. Nonetheless, the experience of time in purgatory is very different from that on earth. One soul in purgatory commented in an apparition: "You cannot understand this, but here in purgatory the time and the intensity of one's pains form a single thing. Our greatest suffering is our nostalgia for God. The more we wait for someone we love, the more slowly the time passes, and the greater is our suffering in this waiting" (*Visions of Purgatory*, p. 152).

In a real sense, purgatory is a manifestation of God's mercy. He shows his mercy both in allowing us to be purified of our sins after death when we should have done this in life, and also for punishing us much less than we deserve for our sins. A young priest in purgatory had this to say to the monk to whom he appeared: "Tell everyone that purgatory was created by merciful love and is the masterpiece of divine mercy and justice. Just one of our sins would merit eternal fire, but the Father does not want his sons to die; he wants their health and their life in him forever... Tell all your brothers that purgatory was created by divine mercy" (*ibid.*, p. 159).

Apparitions from purgatory

There are many books with accounts of souls in purgatory appearing to people on earth. A fairly recent one, which we have already cited, is *Visions of Purgatory*, published in 2014. It gives the account of multiple souls appearing to a monk in the second half of the twentieth century. Another, which we have also used, is *Hungry Souls* by Dutch psychologist Gerard van den Aardweg.

Van den Aardweg describes visiting the modest museum on purgatory in the church of the Sacred Heart of Suffrage very near the Vatican in Rome. The museum was started in 1893 by Fr Victor Jouët, founder of the Archconfraternity of the Sacred Heart of Jesus for Aid to the Holy Souls. At present the museum contains ten items, most of them consisting of burn marks of hands and fingers left by souls from purgatory on books or clothing.

One of the most impressive is the nightshirt of Joseph Leleux. On eleven consecutive nights in 1789 Leleux heard frightening noises in his house in Wodecq, Belgium. Then on June 21 his mother, who had died twenty-seven years before, appeared to him and reminded him that he had an obligation to have Masses celebrated for her soul. She reproached him for his wayward life and begged him to change his ways and work for the Church. Then she laid her hand on the sleeve of his nightshirt, burning into it a clearly marked imprint of her hand. Leleux converted and founded a congregation of pious lay people. He died, with a reputation for holiness, in 1825.

An impressive account in *Hungry Souls* relates the apparitions of a man who died in France in 1870 and appeared numerous times to his daughter, Sister Mary Seraphine, a nun in Malines, Belgium. The account of the apparitions was first published in 1872, and then in 1895 it was included by J.A. Nageleisen in his book *Charity for the Suffering Souls: An Explanation of the Catholic Doctrine of Purgatory* (reprinted by TAN Books, Rockford 1982).

On 27 July 1870 Sr Mary received a letter from France informing her that her father had died on July 17. From that time on she often heard sounds of moaning, like those of her father in his illness, and a voice crying out, "Dear daughter, have mercy on me, have mercy on me, have mercy on me!" On October 14, when she was about to fall asleep, she saw her father standing near her bed, looking very sorrowful and enveloped in flames. She felt as if the flames were scorching her too. From then on she saw her father every evening, except for a few days at the end, until he finally went to heaven.

He explained that the rest of his children thought he was already in heaven and weren't praying for him. This is confirmed by a letter they wrote to their sister: "Father died like a saint and is now in heaven." Only Sr Mary and an old servant named Joanna were praying for him. So the souls in purgatory clearly know who is praying for them – and who is not.

Her father said on one occasion: "Oh, if people would know what purgatory is! They would suffer everything in order to escape it and to release the poor souls confined in it."

He explained that at first he was told he would spend many years in purgatory but that through the intercession of the Blessed Virgin Mary, to whom he had great devotion, his time was reduced to a few months. Nonetheless, his suffering was so intense that he said in October, "If I shall have to remain in purgatory three months more it will seem an eternity." On October 30 he said: "Alas, the world does not believe that the fire of purgatory is similar to that of hell. If a person could but once visit purgatory, he would never more commit the least sin, so rigorously are the souls punished."

On November 30 he told his daughter: "It seems an eternity to me since I arrived in purgatory. At present my greatest torment is the intense longing to behold God and to enjoy his possession." Finally, during Midnight Mass on Christmas Eve he appeared to Sr Mary in great radiance and said: "My punishment is ended. I come to thank you and your community for all the prayers said for me. From now on I shall pray for you all."

What we can we draw from all this? Many things, but especially that purgatory is real. For everyone, not only for Catholics. The soul must be completely purified before it can enter heaven and that is the case for everyone. Purgatory is an exceedingly happy state, but at the same time it is a state of great suffering. We can avoid it by striving, at least from now on, to commit fewer sins and to be truly sorry for them, to do all we can to make up for them by acts of self-denial, deeds of charity, prayers, hard work, etc.

Also, we learn that the souls in purgatory are helped by the prayers of people on earth. Sixteenth-century Lord Chancellor of England St Thomas More, who was later put to death by King

Henry VIII, wrote a brilliant treatise on purgatory titled *The Supplication of Souls*. He writes as if from a soul in purgatory to those on earth, beseeching them to pray for the holy souls. He reminds us how easy it is to forget them: "For if your father, your mother, your child, your brother, your sister, your husband, your wife, or a complete stranger, for that matter, lay within your sight in fire somewhere and you had the means to help them, what heart could be so hard, what stomach so imperturbable, that it could restfully sit at supper or sleep in bed and let a person lie and burn? We therefore find very true that old proverb, 'Out of sight, out of mind'" (Scepter, New York 2002, p. 182). If we believe in prayer, and we pray very much for the souls in purgatory, not only will we help them but, by the justice and mercy of God, we can be sure that, if we go to purgatory ourselves, there will be many people to pray for us.

What is more, by praying for all those who have died, in addition to helping them, we will remind ourselves of the need for this purification of our soul and we will be more likely to avoid purgatory ourselves.

16

Hell

Hell is a frightening prospect. It means eternal separation from the God for whom we were made and from his love, a love which can fill us with joy and peace more than we can possibly imagine. At the same time it means eternal punishment, likened to fire. That is indeed daunting, something no one would want to experience.

Wherever did we get the idea of hell? Really, there is a deep-seated sense in all of us that there should be justice, that good deeds should be rewarded and evil ones punished. And since this does not always happen here on earth, our sense of justice argues that if there is life after death at least it should happen in the next life. That does not prove that there is a hell, but it does respond to our natural desire for justice that it would be good if there was one. For someone else, of course, not for ourselves.

Hell in the Scriptures

Actually, it was Jesus Christ himself who told us about hell. Many times. In his description of the judgment he speaks of the Son of man coming in his glory and gathering before him all the nations, separating them as the shepherd separates the sheep from the goats. After describing the reward of eternal life to be given to the righteous, he says to the others: "Depart from me, you cursed, into the eternal fire prepared for the devil and his angels; for I was hungry and you gave me no food, I was thirsty and you gave me no drink... And they will go away into eternal punishment, but the righteous into eternal life" (*Matt* 25:31-46).

In this passage Christ mentions the two principal forms of punishment in hell. In saying "Depart from me" he is speaking of the eternal separation of the soul from God, known as the "pain of loss". And in "the eternal fire prepared for the devil and his angels" he is speaking of the "pain of sense". Even though it is experienced only in the soul, the pain is exceedingly intense, likened to fire in many passages of the Bible. And, of course, the punishment of hell is eternal, forever.

If the pain of fire sounds great, the pain of not being with God is greater. St John Chrysostom, who died in 407 AD, writes: "Unbearable is the fire of hell – who does not know it? – and dreadful are its torments; but, if one were to heap a thousand hell-fires one on the other, it would be as nothing compared with the punishment of being excluded from the blessed glory of heaven ... and of being compelled to hear Christ say: 'I know you not'" (*Homilies on Matthew,* 23, 9).

So it is Jesus himself, who loves us so much that he died on the cross for us and who wants all to be saved, who speaks of eternal punishment. Moreover, he makes it clear that it is easy to go to hell: "Enter by the narrow gate; for the gate is wide and the way is easy, that leads to destruction, and those who enter by it are many. For the gate is narrow and the way is hard, that leads to life, and those who find it are few" (*Matthew* 7:13-14).

By these words Jesus seems to be saying that it is much easier to go to hell, to "destruction", than to heaven, to "life". If we think about it, we would probably agree. We all have a natural tendency to do the wrong thing: to be proud, self-centred, lazy, deceitful, unkind, dishonest, greedy, etc. And we know well that unless we struggle to resist these tendencies, we can easily fall into a way of life that is seriously disordered, in which we do grave harm to ourselves and others. If we are not sorry for these offences and we do nothing to repair the damage we have caused, we could go to hell.

Hell in the teaching of the Church

Jesus' teaching, then, is clear. But does the Church still believe in hell? Of course it does. It has always believed in hell. According to the *Catechism of the Catholic Church*, "The teaching of the Church affirms the existence of hell and its eternity. Immediately after death the souls of those who die in a state of mortal sin descend into hell, where they suffer the punishments of hell, 'eternal fire'. The chief punishment of hell is eternal separation from God, in whom alone man can possess the life and happiness for which he was created and for which he longs" (*CCC* 1035). By "mortal sin", the Catechism means serious, grave sin, such as murder, adultery, theft of a large sum of money, etc. The word "mortal", by the way, comes from the Latin word for death. Mortal sin is death-dealing to the soul.

The Second Vatican Council declared: "Since we know neither the day nor the hour, we should follow the advice of the Lord and watch constantly so that, when the single course of our earthly life is completed, we may merit to enter with him into the marriage feast and be numbered among the blessed and not, like the wicked and slothful servants, be ordered to depart into the eternal fire, into the outer darkness where men will weep and gnash their teeth" (*LG* 48).

But, we might ask, how can a good God send anyone to eternal punishment? The answer is simple. He doesn't. God doesn't send anyone to hell. On the contrary, he wants all to be saved and to come to the knowledge of the truth (cf. *1 Tim* 2:4), and he gives everyone sufficient help, or grace, to be saved (cf. *2 Cor* 12:9). It is the person who sends himself, or herself, to hell. We saw this in the near-death experience of those who found themselves going to hell. They acknowledged that they were not sent there against their wishes, but rather it was their own free choices that got them there.

The Catechism puts it like this: "To die in mortal sin without repenting and accepting God's merciful love means remaining separated from him forever by our own free choice. This state of definitive self-exclusion from communion with God and the blessed is called 'hell'" (*CCC* 1033).

As this point implies, all someone needs to do to escape hell and go to heaven is to be sorry for their sins, especially the serious ones, the mortal sins. This is not difficult. When the person is truly sorry, he accepts the merciful love of God, who is always ready to forgive the sinner. If, however, he remains obstinate in his sins, without being sorry, he is in effect choosing hell.

Hell and sorrow for sin

One person who had just such an experience is Fr Steven Scheier, an American priest, who was ordained in 1973 and had a serious car accident in 1985. In a head-on collision with another vehicle, he was thrown onto the pavement, and was left unconscious and seriously injured. The scalp on the right side of his head was torn off, part of his brain was sheared off, many brain cells were crushed, and he had a broken vertebra in his neck. He was given a fifteen per cent chance of survival.

While unconscious, he had a near-death experience in which he found himself before Jesus Christ in the judgment. He saw his sins, which he acknowledges were "unrepented, unconfessed and unforgiven". He says he always had excuses when he committed those sins, but "when talking to Truth personified, alone before the judgment seat, excuses don't exist. No rebuttal is possible. To each offense, I easily agreed. The only thing I could do when Jesus spoke about particular instances in my life was to say internally, 'Yes ... Yes, that's true.' When the Lord finished, he said, 'The sentence that you will have for all eternity is hell.' I knew before he even said it what my fate would be. Jesus was doing nothing but honoring my decision. 'I know this is what I deserve,' I thought. ...Then another voice that filled me with horror said, 'Come on down. You belong to me.'"

Fr Scheier goes on to relate how he then heard a female voice, the softest and sweetest voice he had ever heard, obviously of Jesus' mother Mary, who begged Jesus to spare his life and immortal soul. "The Lord then said, 'Mother, he has been a priest for twelve years for himself and not for Me. Let him reap the punishment he deserves.' At that, I heard her say again in response, 'But Son, if we give to him special graces and strengths and come to him in ways that he is not familiar with, we can see if he bears fruit. If he does not, then Your will be done.' There was a short pause, which seemed like an eternity. Then His voice came back and said, 'Mother, he's yours.'" (*The Warning,* Queen of Peace Media, 2019, pp. 71-72). Needless to say, when Fr Scheier recovered, he repented and became a very zealous priest.

But couldn't God take everyone to heaven? He could. But it would mean not respecting the freedom he gave us, and God is too much of a father to do that. The then Cardinal Joseph Ratzinger, later Pope Benedict XVI, explains: "God never, in any case, forces anyone to be saved. God accepts man's freedom. He is no magician, who will in the end wipe out everything that has happened and wheel out his happy ending. He is a true father; a creator who assents to freedom, even when it is used to reject him. That is why God's all-embracing desire to save people does not involve the actual salvation of all men. He allows us the power to refuse. God loves us; we need only to summon up the humility to allow ourselves to be loved" (*God is Near Us,* Ignatius 2003, pp. 36-37).

The British writer C.S. Lewis says something similar in his book *The Great Divorce* (1945), speaking about the end of life: "There are only two kinds of people in the end: those who say to God, 'Thy will be done', and those to whom God says, in the end, 'Thy will be done'. All that are in hell choose it. Without that self-choice there could be no hell. No soul that seriously and constantly desires joy will ever miss it. Those who seek find. To those who knock it is opened" (p. 58).

God could not have done more to keep us out of hell. He sent his eternal Son to become man in Jesus Christ, who suffered and died on a cross to open for us the way to heaven. Christ told us about the reality of hell so that we would be warned of what awaits us if we die without sorrow for our sins. He gives us all the help we need throughout our life to do what is right and avoid doing what is wrong. He is always ready to forgive us when we come to him with true sorrow for our sins. He could not do more. Now it is up to us.

What then can we do to avoid going to hell? First, and most importantly, be truly sorry for our sins and resolve to lead a better life. The Catechism says: "The affirmations of Sacred Scripture and the teachings of the Church on the subject of hell are a call to the responsibility incumbent upon man to make use of his freedom in view of his eternal destiny. They are at the same time an urgent call to conversion: 'Enter by the narrow gate; for the gate is wide and the way is easy, that leads to destruction, and those who enter by it are many. For the gate is narrow and the way is hard, that leads to life, and those who find it are few' (*Matt* 7:13-14; *CCC* 1036).

Can we say, as some do, that God predestines some to hell and others to heaven? We can never say that. He made us free and he respects our freedom. In the words of the Catechism, "God predestines no one to go to hell; for this a wilful turning away from God (a mortal sin) is necessary, and persistence in it until the end. In the Eucharistic liturgy and in the daily prayers of her faithful, the Church implores the mercy of God, who does not want 'any to perish, but all to come to repentance" (*2 Pet* 3:9; *CCC* 1037).

The experience of hell

As regards the suffering of those in hell, it will be helpful to hear just a little of the experience of a Spanish nun who was allowed to experience that suffering first-hand various times. Sister Josefa Menendez was born in Madrid in 1890 and in 1920 she entered the French convent of Les Feuillants in Poitiers as a Coadjutrix Sister of the Society of the Sacred Heart. She died there less than four years later in the fame of sanctity, and the process of the recognition of her sainthood by the Church has been opened. She had many revelations from Jesus Christ and his mother Mary, which she wrote down in her book *The Way of Divine Love.*

Sr Josefa repeatedly dwelt on what she described as the greatest torment of hell, the soul's inability to love. She writes: "One of these damned souls cried out: 'This is my torture... that I want to love and cannot; there is nothing left to me but hatred and despair. If one of us could so much as make a single act of love... This would no longer be hell... but we cannot, we live on hatred and malevolence.'" Another soul cried out: "The greatest of our torments here is that we are not able to love him. While we hunger for love, we are consumed with desire of it, but it is too late" (23

March 1922).

She witnessed too the accusations the souls in hell make against themselves: "Some yell because of the martyrdom of their hands. Perhaps they were thieves, for they say: 'Where is our loot now?' ... Cursed hands ... Others curse their tongues, their eyes ... whatever was the occasion of sin ... 'Now, O body, you are paying the price of the delights you granted yourself! ... and you did it of your own free will...'" (2 April 1922).

This is combined with Christ's ardent desire to save souls from going to hell. He told Sr Josefa: "Help me; help me to make my love for men known, for I come to tell them that in vain will they seek happiness apart from me, for they will not find it. Suffer, Josefa, and love, for we two must win these souls" (13 June 1923).

As regards the mercy of God in forgiving repentant sinners, she records these words from Jesus: "I would like [those living with sin] to understand that it is not the fact of being in sin that ought to keep them from me. They must never think that there is no remedy for them, nor that they have forfeited forever the love that once was theirs... No, poor souls, the God who has shed all his Blood for you has no such feelings for you." As Jesus says, it is not the fact of sin that keeps people from God, but the lack of sorrow. God is merciful and he will always forgive us. All we need to do is ask him for forgiveness.

Another person who experienced hell is Bill Wiese, an American real estate broker, who had an out-of-body experience in November, 1998, which he relates in his book *23 Minutes in Hell* (Charisma House, 2006). The book was a New York Times bestseller, which sold over one million copies. Wiese describes the torment of fire, the horrible demons, the anguish of other souls in hell and above all, the hopelessness one experiences there. He then encountered Jesus, who told him to tell other people that hell is real. Wiese says that his experience ended with him lying on the floor of his living room, screaming in horror.

From all of this it is clear that hell, like heaven, is real. It exists. We saw this too on considering near-death experiences, where some persons had a "hellish" experience of suffering, to warn them of what they would deserve if they didn't amend their ways. If we need more convincing, the book *Hungry Souls* by Dutch psychologist Gerard van den Aardweg has two accounts of souls in hell appearing to friends on earth.

The author takes the accounts from the little book *Hell*, written by Bishop Louis Gaston de Ségur (1820-1881) of Saint-Denis, Paris, in 1876. Bishop de Ségur was descended on his father's side from the Marquis of Ségur, Marshal of France and Minister of Louis XVI, and on his mother's side from the Russian Count Rostopchine, who burned Moscow in 1812 in order to wrest it from Napoleon. Count Rostopchine, Bishop de Ségur's grandfather, was a close friend of Russian General Count Orloff, a protagonist in the first of the following two stories, giving it great credibility.

Shortly before 1812, General Orloff and another man, identified as General V., were ridiculing religion, especially hell, at a dinner and they agreed that, if by chance there was life after death, whichever of them died first would come back to tell the other about it. Some weeks later General V. was sent to the front to take up an important command in the war then raging against Napoleon. Early one morning several weeks later, General Orloff suddenly burst into the room of Count Rostopchine, looking pale and greatly disturbed. He explained that he had been lying in bed when suddenly General V. appeared in the room, standing upright and pale, with his right hand on his chest and saying, "There is a hell and I am there!" Then he disappeared. Ten or twelve days later an army messenger brought the news that General V. had been shot in the chest and killed at the very hour he appeared to Count Orloff.

When Bishop de Ségur told this story to the Superior of a religious community of men in 1859, the latter related another story told to him by a relative of the woman protagonist, who was then still alive. This woman, who was a widow of about twenty-nine years of age at the time, was in London in the winter of 1847 to 1848. She was very worldly, wealthy and attractive, and was sinning with a young man. One night around one in the morning, as she was falling asleep, a glimmer of light appeared at the door of her room, and it gradually became brighter and larger. Then she saw the door open slowly. It was the young man, who entered and came over to her. He took her by the left wrist and said, "There is a hell." The pain in her wrist was so great that she passed out.

A half hour later she came to and called for her chambermaid, who noticed the smell of burning when she entered the room. She looked at the woman's wrist and saw a burn mark the size of a man's hand so deep that the bone was laid bare. What is more, the carpet was burned with the imprint of a man's steps from the door to the bed and back again. The next day the woman learned that the man had died at the same time he appeared to her. After that the woman wore a broad gold bracelet to cover the burn mark.

While these accounts can be frightening, they have every probability of being true. They speak to us of the existence of hell and of the possibility of people who have died going there and of their appearing afterwards on earth to tell us about it. Are we required to believe in hell, based on these accounts? That is up to each one. We don't have to believe them. But we would be very foolish to ignore them, or especially to deny the existence of hell. Very foolish indeed.

All of this leads us to our next and final topic: what must we do to prepare for the day when we too, of necessity, will die and face God in our judgment, so that we can merit eternal life with him in heaven?

17

What must I do?

A s we have seen repeatedly throughout this little book, there is life after death, whether we believe in it or not. We have a spiritual soul and that soul cannot be destroyed. It lives on necessarily, in some form of existence.

We have seen too, both from the thousands of cases of near-death experiences and from the revelation God has given us through Jesus Christ and his Church, that one of the possible states of the soul after death is heaven. Heaven is a state of indescribable happiness, of unalloyed peace and love, and it is forever. What is more, heaven is what God wants for all of us. Christ became man and died for us to open up the way to heaven. He has gone ahead to prepare a place for us in his Father's house. He wants us to join him there, along with the angels and countless persons who have already arrived there, including many of our relatives and friends.

If our soul needs purification before it is ready for heaven, and that is quite likely for most of us, it will be cleansed in the purifying fire of God's love in purgatory. There we will be exceedingly happy, as we are assured of heaven and closer to God than we are on earth, at the same time as we will suffer until our purification is complete.

And, of course, there is the possibility of hell, the state of separation from God and of great pain. It too is forever. Forever. We don't want to go there.

So the big question is: What must I do? What must I do to deserve heaven? The very fact that you ask the question is already a start. You want to know how to change your life so that when you die you will be deserving of eternal life with God. You are looking for the answer. You are searching.

A God of love and mercy

Perhaps the first part of the answer is to know that the God who wants to take you with him to heaven is a God of love, of mercy. By the way, this God is your God, no matter what religion you may have or have had in the past. There is only God and he is the God, indeed the Father, of all.

Sometimes people conceive of God as a God of anger, ever ready to punish, as if he made human beings so that he could make them suffer. But God is not like that. The Scriptures describe him as a God who is "ever rich in mercy". In the Old Testament book of Exodus, God describes himself as "a God merciful and gracious, slow to anger, and abounding in mercy and faithfulness, keeping merciful love for thousands, forgiving iniquity and transgression and sin" (*Exodus* 34:5-7). The prophet Isaiah describes God's mercy in graphic terms: "Can a woman forget her sucking child, that she should have no compassion on the son of her womb? Even these may forget, yet I will not forget you. Behold, I have carved you on the palms of my hands" (*Isaiah* 49:15-16).

Jesus Christ himself forgave many sinners, including a woman caught in the act of adultery. To make it easy for people to have their sins forgiven, he gave his Church a way for priests to forgive sins in his name: the sacrament of Penance, or Confession. And he gave us the beautiful parable, or story, of the prodigal son. It involves a young man who asked his father for the share of inheritance that was his, so he could go away and explore a different lifestyle. The father gave him the money and he left. But, as his father no doubt feared, he fell in with the wrong company and spent all his money on a life of sin with women. Now without any money, he was given a job feeding pigs, and he saw that the pigs had more to eat than he did. He then decided to go back to his father and tell him he was sorry for what he had done, asking to be taken back, not as a son but as a hired servant. To his joy, when his father saw him coming he ran out, embraced and kissed him and prepared a fatted calf for a meal to celebrate his son's homecoming. This is an image of God, the merciful father, who will always take back a son or daughter of his who returns with sorrow for what they have done, no matter how many sins they have committed (cf. *Luke* 15:11-32).

And St Paul, in his letter to those in Ephesus, reminds us how, when we were sunk in our sins, God in his mercy raised us up:

> And you he made alive, when you were dead through the trespasses and sins in which you once walked, following the course of this world, following the prince of the power of the air, the spirit that is now at work in the sons of disobedience. Among these we all once lived in the passions of our flesh, following the desires of body and mind, and so we were by nature children of wrath, like the rest of mankind. But God, who is rich in mercy, out of the great love with which he loved us, even when we were dead through our trespasses, made us alive together with Christ (by grace you have been saved), and raised us up with him, and made us sit with him in the heavenly places in Christ Jesus, that in the coming ages he might show the immeasurable riches of his grace in kindness toward us in Christ Jesus (*Eph* 2:1-7).

This is the God who created us and who wants us to be with him forever in heaven. He is a God of mercy, ever ready to forgive. He wants our eternal salvation more than we do. He loves us more than we love ourselves. St John goes so far as to say that "God is love" (*1 John* 4:8). He will do anything to take us to heaven.

A beautiful story of God's mercy is that of a man who was known as a great sinner and whom everyone thought went to hell when he died. In life he had despised religion and he was known as a libertine, unscrupulous, hard on his employees and his family, and a gambler. He died suddenly in an accident and not even the members of his family prayed for him, thinking he had gone to hell. More than twenty-five years later he appeared from purgatory to a monk who had known him and was surprised at his apparition. He explained that he had been saved by the prayers of the many people he had helped on earth through his almsgiving, giving anonymously so that no one would know who had helped them (cf. *Visions from Purgatory,* pp. 177-178). Yes, God will offer his mercy to everyone. He wants all to be saved.

Sorrow for our sins

So we don't need to fear God. He loves us and he wants us to be with him. What then must we do? The first, and most important thing, is to be sorry for our sins, for our offences against him and against others. We recall what we read about those who go to hell: "To die in mortal sin without repenting and accepting God's merciful love means remaining separated from him for ever by our own free choice: (*CCC* 1033). In simple terms, if we repent of our sins and accept God's merciful love, which will always be offered us, we will not go to hell. We will go to heaven.

But what must we be sorry for? We all have a sense that many of the things we have done during our life were wrong. Perhaps they hurt someone else and we were keenly aware of it at the time. Maybe they even broke up a marriage, or broke off an important relationship, or cost us our job. It can be helpful to recall those many near-death experiences in which the person was allowed to feel what the other person felt when the first person offended them. That would be a powerful experience. Hopefully, we apologised at the time to those we hurt. If we didn't, we can still do it now. And, especially, we should tell God we are sorry.

We may also have committed offences against our marriage and family: being unfaithful to our spouse, having recourse to prostitution, viewing pornography, being abusive to family members, not giving our spouse the time and attention they needed, being away from the family for long periods of time without a sufficient reason, not spending enough time with our children. As we go through life, we may tend to regard some of our offences as being of little importance. But when we look back on them from a distance, seeing the negative consequences they had, we realise they were more important than we thought at the time. This moves us to be truly sorry for them, and to tell this to God.

There may have been offences against life itself, ours or someone else's. The worst, of course, is taking or harming the life of an innocent person. This may be through abortion, reckless driving occasioning death or grievous bodily harm, injuring someone in a fight, encouraging someone to take drugs which damaged their health or life, etc. Similarly, we may have harmed our own health or life by drinking habitually to excess, taking illicit drugs, not following a prescribed diet for a medical condition, not taking prescribed medicines...

Or offences against justice: failing to pay workers what was due them, stealing, damaging another's property, not returning borrowed goods, not paying taxes...

And we may have told lies that caused serious harm to someone, or damaged another's good reputation by spreading gossip or lies about them.

These are just a few of the many things we may have done wrong in our life. They may help to jog our memory and so recall others. In any case, we should remember that we will be judged by God according to his standard, not our own. When we appear before him in the judgment, we will see clearly our whole life as God sees and judges it. It will be the moment of truth. For this reason we want to acknowledge our faults and change our life now, while there is still time. In the judgment it will be too late.

If we have any doubts about what is right and wrong, we can talk with someone who is more familiar with God's law than we are. Or we can read a book about morality which explains the main faults, based on the Ten Commandments which God gave to Moses in the Old Testament (cf. *Exodus* 20:1-17). The *Catechism of the Catholic Church* is a good start, or the shorter *Compendium* of the Catechism.

As we look back on our life and see the many things we have done wrong, we are naturally moved to be sorry for them. This sorrow must be genuine, with a true conversion of heart, even when it comes at the very end of life. As the Catechism puts it, "Interior repentance is a radical reorientation of our whole life, a return, a conversion to God with all our heart, an end of sin, a turning away from evil, with repugnance towards the evil actions we have committed. At the same time it entails the desire and resolution to change one's life, with hope in God's mercy and trust in the help of his grace" (*CCC* 1431). Although we may not experience all of this, it is clear that repentance must be a real conversion of heart, a rejection of sin, not just a passing thought or sentiment.

We can be sure that God will give us all the help we need to have this sorrow and desire of conversion. The Catechism explains: "Conversion is first of all a work of the grace of God who makes our hearts return to him: 'Restore us to thyself, O Lord, that we may be restored!' God gives us the strength to begin anew" (*Lam* 5:21; *CCC* 1432).

Naturally, conversion must also involve our free response to that divine help: "It is in discovering the greatness of God's love that our heart is shaken by the horror and weight of sin and begins to fear offending God by sin and being separated from him. The human heart is converted by looking upon him whom our sins have pierced" (*CCC* 1432).

When God sees our sorrow, our repentance and desire to change, his merciful love will move him to forgive us. Sometimes it may be at the very last moment of life that he grants the gift of repentance. This was the case with the father of an Australian priest who did not accept his son's vocation to the priesthood and was hostile towards him. When the father was dying, the son went to visit him in the hope that his father might be reconciled with him and accept his vocation, at least before he died. But when the priest was there beside the bed, his father leaned forward, spat in his son's face and said: "That's what I think of you and your Church." He leaned back and died.

After that, the son lived with the fear that his father may have gone to hell. Then one day, sometime later, the priest was visiting a monastery of Carmelite nuns. While he was speaking with one of the nuns, another nun was in the chapel praying. She may not have known that the priest was even there or, if she did, she would certainly not have known what had happened between him and his father. In any case, in some way she heard Christ say to her: "Go and tell the priest that before his father died, he saw me on the cross and begged forgiveness for his sins, and he is now in purgatory. She told this to the priest, who was greatly relieved that his father was on his way to heaven.

Recently, a lawyer friend told me another story of God's mercy at the end of life. The lawyer had a client who came to him to contest his father's will. It seems that the client's father, of a religious background but with atheistic views, left his wife and young son when the boy was just a child. When he grew up, the son adopted a homosexual lifestyle and became a dancer. When his father died and had not included him in his will, the son sought help from the lawyer to contest the will. But now the son was dying of HIV-AIDS, and he called the lawyer to his bedside, not for legal advice, but just to talk. He obviously regarded the lawyer as a friend.

Sometime later, the man was at the end of his life and his mother called the lawyer to visit him. He went and found the patient unresponsive, with an oxygen mask over his nose and mouth. He began to talk to him, knowing that the last sense to leave a dying person is that of hearing. He then remembered that that morning he had been in a Mass in which the priest told the people: "Remember, no matter what you have done, Jesus loves you." The lawyer said this to the man, holding his hand at the same time. When he said it, the man squeezed his hand tightly and held it for a long time. The following day the mother rang the lawyer to tell him that just after he left, her son had died.

You can make of this what you will. Personally, I like to think that the God of love and mercy inspired the lawyer to say what he did as a way of moving that man to be reconciled with God at the very last moment. It didn't make any difference how many sins he had committed during his lifetime. If he was sorry for them, the God who loved him and wanted to take him with him, would forgive him.

Yes, God can give the grace of repentance and salvation at the very end of someone's life. But we should not count on that. Now is the time for sorrow, so that we can be well prepared to meet God when he calls us into the next life.

Forgiving others

As we approach the end of life, we also reflect more seriously on other things we must attend to before we make our departure. This can take many forms.

An important one is to forgive from the bottom of our heart anyone who has offended us. Looking back over our life we may remember certain people who have hurt us, or who have hurt others close to us, badly. When we think of them, we may still feel angry towards them. But we don't want to go to our grave without forgiving them.

Jesus Christ, whom we hope to see and be with for all eternity, spoke in the Sermon on the Mount about the importance of forgiving. It was there that he gave us the Lord's Prayer, the Our Father, in which we say: "Forgive us our trespasses as we forgive those who trespass against us." As these words imply, we must forgive those who have hurt us if we expect God to forgive us our trespasses, our sins. Immediately after giving us the Our Father, Jesus went on to say: "For if you forgive men their trespasses, your heavenly Father also will forgive you; but if you do not forgive men their trespasses, neither will your Father forgive your trespasses" (*Matthew* 6:14-15). These are strong words and a reminder of the importance of forgiving.

To explain this teaching, Christ gave us the parable of a servant who owed his master ten thousand talents, an enormous sum of money, millions of dollars in today's terms. When he pleaded to be given time to pay, the master forgave him the whole debt. But even after that the servant was unwilling to show mercy to a fellow servant who owed him just one hundred denarii, equivalent to a hundred days' wages of an unskilled worker. In anger, the master ordered the first servant to be put in jail until he paid the whole amount. Jesus added: "So also my heavenly Father will do to every one of you, if you do not forgive your brother from your heart" (*Matthew* 18:23-35). We are the servant who has been forgiven so much by God and is unwilling to forgive our fellow man a slight offence. No matter how much someone may have offended us, it is nothing compared to how much we have offended God. So, if God has forgiven us the great debt of our sins against him, we should forgive others the much smaller debt of their offences against us.

And we must be ready to forgive our neighbour not once or twice, but always. On one occasion Peter asked Jesus how often he should forgive his brother, if as many as seven times. Jesus answered: "I do not say to you seven times, but seventy times seven" (*Matthew* 18:22). Seven is the number of plenitude, of fulness, in the Scriptures. It means an indefinite number. So we must be ready to forgive our neighbour always, no matter how many times he offends us.

But what does it mean to forgive? To forgive is to tell God, and ideally also the one who has hurt us, that we don't hold anything against them, that we wish them well, not harm, that we love them, that we pray for them. Forgiveness is an act of the will, relieving the other person of any debt against us. It is not a spontaneous feeling of kindness towards the person. When we think of what they have done, we will probably feel angry for quite some time. This is not a sign that we have not forgiven, but simply a natural response of our nature.

On the other hand, we should try to reject quickly any thoughts of the offence the person has committed against us, since these thoughts can reopen the wound and prolong the hard feelings. The sooner we get over reminding ourselves of the offence, the better.

They say, "forgive and forget". But while we can always forgive, it is not easy to forget, nor is forgetting necessary for our forgiveness to be genuine. At the same time, it is also true that the less we think about the offence, the more quickly we will forget it.

But, you might ask, are we to forgive someone who is not sorry for the hurt they have caused us? This can often be the case. It is harder to forgive such a person, but the answer would seem to be clearly yes, we should forgive them. Christ does not make any distinction when he tells us we must forgive others if we want God to forgive us. Then too, Christ gives us his own example of forgiving people who were not sorry for having offended him. On the cross of Calvary, he asked the Father to forgive those who were crucifying him, saying: "Father, forgive them; for they know not what they do" (*Luke* 23:34). It is almost certain that among those who were crucifying Jesus there were some – perhaps many – who were not sorry at all for what they were doing. But Jesus still asked the Father to forgive them. When he asks us to love one another as he has loved us (cf. *John* 13:34) he is undoubtedly asking us to forgive those who are not sorry for having hurt us, just as he asks the Father to forgive those who have hurt him.

We should remember too that we can never be certain that the other person is not sorry. We should always give them the benefit of the doubt. It is a source of great joy and peace to forgive someone who has hurt us. Indeed, one of the last lines in the beautiful Roland Joffé film *There be Dragons* about St Josemaría Escrivá is: "When you forgive, you set someone free – yourself."

Drawing closer to God

Is there anything else you should do to prepare for your encounter with God? Yes, there is, and it is very much a matter of where you are now in your relationship with him.

The first thing, and this applies to everyone, is to make an effort, a real effort, to be a better person from now on. If you have managed to find the way to be sorry for your sins, that in itself implies that you are prepared to do everything you can to avoid committing those sins in the future. If you have this attitude, you are off to a good start. Even though your past might be something of a horror story, don't worry. God forgives all of that and wipes the slate clean. The rest of your life can still be a love story, even though it might be relatively short. By showing more love and kindness to those around you, you are in effect showing love to God too. Jesus said as much, referring to all the acts of charity we have shown others: "Truly, I say to you, as you did it to one of the least of these my brethren, you did it to me" (*Matthew* 25:40). And, of course, you are likely to fall again into some of your sins. Don't worry. Just tell God you are sorry and start over. That is the story of everyone's life. Beginning and beginning again.

Also, since you are preparing to meet God, you can make an effort to get to know him better. Read about him, using whatever books you find helpful. If you have some religion in your life, or at least you have had it in the past, go back to the religious texts of your earlier days and read them again. They will lead you to know God better and to have a more personal relationship with him. If your religion is Christianity, the obvious book is the Bible. Go back and read it again, especially the New Testament. Also very helpful are books about the life of Christ.

Your personal relationship is expressed in many ways but one of the most simple, and obvious, is prayer. What is prayer? It is simply to talk with God, and to listen to him. You can tell him that you love him, ask him for favours, thank him for the many blessings he has granted you throughout your life, and tell him you are sorry for your offences against him. Also, many religions have prayers that are commonly said by all members of that religion.

If that is your case and you are familiar with those prayers, by all means go back and say them again. The important thing is to establish a personal relationship with the God you are going to meet when you die. You want to be on familiar terms with him.

If you belong to some religious faith, it may have regular services dedicated to the worship of God. If that is the case, by all means go to those services. They will help you to honour the God you are going to meet and to prepare you for that encounter. They will also put you in contact with other people who will support you on your journey. If you haven't been to such services for a long time, perhaps for many years or even decades, don't be afraid. Go back and pick up where you left off. It is most likely that you will be warmly welcomed back into that religious family.

And if your religion is Catholic or Orthodox, or any other faith which has the rite of confession of sins, take advantage of that rite to confess your sins and purify your soul. You will have the joy of the prodigal son of whom we heard a few pages ago. It was no doubt very difficult for that young man to admit his failings and unworthiness to his father, but he was welcomed back with great joy. That joy can be yours when you confess your sins with humility and sorrow.

With all of this preparation, you need not fear death nor what happens to you afterwards. You can look forward to it with great hope and confidence. Death will come – for all of us – but, as we have seen, if we live and die well, there is life after death and it promises indescribable happiness, love and peace – for all eternity. God is a loving and merciful Father and he has prepared a room for everyone in his house. If we live the rest of our life well, we can look forward to going home to heaven, where we will be with God forever.

I look forward to meeting you there. And, oh, if you believe in prayer, please pray for me, so that I get there too.

www.ingramcontent.com/pod-product-compliance
Lightning Source LLC
LaVergne TN
LVHW041631190225
804056LV00009B/116